# Stumbling
# Toward
# Enlightenment

## GERI LARKIN

CELESTIAL ARTS

BERKELEY, CALIFORNIA

Celestial Arts Publishing
P.O. Box 7123
Berkeley, California 94707

Grateful acknowledgement is made for permission to reprint excerpts
from *The Dhammapada: The Sayings of the Buddha* by Thomas Byron,
translator, copyright ©1976 by Thomas Byron. Reprinted by
permission of Alfred A. Knopf, Inc.

Celestial Arts titles are distributed in Canada by Publisher's Group West,
in the United Kingdom and Europe by Airlift Books, in South Africa by
Real Books, in New Zealand by Tandem Press, and by Berkeley Books.

Cover Photo: Chantra Pramkaew
Cover Design: Brad Greene
Text Design: Shelley Firth

Printed in the United States
Library of Congress Cataloging-in-Publication Data

Larkin, Geri.
Stumbling toward enlightenment / Geri Larkin.
p.  cm.
ISBN 0-89087-849-8 (paper)
1. Larkin, Geri   2. Spiritual life—Buddhism.
3. Spiritual biography United States   I. Title.
BQ970.A556A3   1997
294.3'44'092—dc21          97-21858   CIP
[B]

First Printing, 1997
2 3 4 5 6 7 / 04  03  02  01  99  98  97

# Dedication

*This book is dedicated to my teachers*
*Venerable Samu Sunim and Reverend Sukha Linda Murray.*
*Without their faith and hard work*
*I would be somebody.*

*And to Karen Aldridge*
*because she has more courage and more tenacity*
*that anyone else I know.*

# Contents

# Foreword

Each of us has a yearning for the divine. When we decide to do something about this yearning—such as going back to church, or finally starting to pay attention in church, or shifting our work so it better matches our deepest values, or even reading about spiritual topics—we have, whether we are fully conscious of it or not, embarked on a spiritual path.

When we enter this path, most of us believe that it will be a pretty straight road, not necessarily easy, but at least straight. For most of us, however, the reality is that spiritual growth is like learning to walk. We stand up, fall, stand up, fall, take a step, fall, take a couple of steps, fall, walk a little better, wobble a bit, fall, run, walk, and finally, eventually fly. Sometimes we slide backwards after every step forward. And sometimes we find ourselves head first in a bush by the roadside, blocked by a boulder in the middle of the path, stuck until we can figure our way through. It's *never* a straight line.

*Stumbling Toward Enlightenment* is my promise to stand right beside you, wobbling right along, sharing the teachings that have helped us and so many others walk a little straighter, fly a little sooner. My anchor is *The Dhammapada*, perhaps the best known collection of the Buddha's teachings. Made up of twenty-six chapters, *The Dhammapada* offers up the core themes of *mindfulness* and *loving kindness* in teachings that range from the implications of the choices we make to guidelines for tasting happiness in the midst of everyday dreariness, or what I like to call accessible Zen.

Building from the teachings of *The Dhammapada*, this book offers stories and guidance for people who are starting to explore their spirituality more deeply and want to taste Buddhism without feeling obligated to know its history and constructs. There are lessons related to the impact of the choices we make in our lives; the importance of being aware; the dangers of grasping at pleasures; and the components of real wisdom.

The style is painfully honest (for me anyway), earthy, and maybe even a bit scrappy. Real life stories, sprinkled with dharma wisdom from ancient Zen masters, illustrate the teachings. My goal is simple: to encourage each of you to enter your own spiritual forest, head held high, or to travel further into the one you have chosen, leaving fear behind.

This book grew out of requests for written copies of the dharma talks I gave at the Ann Arbor Zen Buddhist Temple and The Chicago Zen Buddhist Temple in 1995 and 1996. So regularly would people approach me after the talks and ask for a copy of my notes, which were at best illegible, and at worst, utterly unrelated to what I had spoken about, that I finally decided to get them down on paper in a reasonably organized and, hopefully, useful way. Have fun with them.

Here are my thank-yous: To Alan Richter, who introduced me to Andrea Pedolsky, who introduced me to David Hinds and Veronica Randall at Celestial Arts. Full-bodied Bodhisattvas, I say. To Buddha who started this ball of doubt rolling in the first place, and to my mother who didn't need to be convinced, after all, that I had fallen into the hands of a cult. The biggest thank-you of all goes to you, the reader, for your open admission of your spiritual side and the courage you have shown in considering that there might be more that you can do. There is.

# Chapter One

# If I Can, You Can

---

### *A ZEN FABLE*

*In China there was a Zen master who spent his time traveling throughout the countryside, visiting different temples, always accompanied by a handful of disciples who were very proud of their master. One day they camped near a river. Looking downriver they noticed another group of monks. At the same moment, a member of the other group noticed the master and his disciples and walked along the path until he reached one of the master's disciples. As he stood facing the river, he asked if the wandering master could do any magic tricks. He said his own master was particularly talented and in fact, could stand on this side of the river and write characters in the air, and if someone was standing on the other side of the river with a piece of paper in their hand the characters would appear on the sheet of paper. The monk listening to him replied that his master was also very talented, capable of performing the most amazing things. For example, if he slept, he slept and if he ate, he ate. Humbled, his visitor walked back to his group, determined to learn to master such feats even if it took him ten thousand lifetimes.*

---

So, here's how I got started. For years I was a card-carrying nothing. I was just too busy living my life to even consider whether there was a God or which particular Goddess started my family line. Four high school years in an Australian boarding school for young women run by Catholic nuns taught me that the Pope and I would never agree on enough to make me a Catholic, although I loved the rituals and the nuns. They were the only calm people I ever met until I hit my thirties. In fact, the years I lived in New York City while I was in college taught me that the world is so hyper that I wondered whether the nuns had been real or an illusion.

My mother taught me that wisdom doesn't need to come from "religion," and my father taught me that my life's work was to work hard, get rich, and marry a good-looking man. Since he was the stronger influence, I worked myself to the bone, made enough money to own a big brick house and drive a Saab, and marry several really good-looking men in succession. (Can you see how the Pope and I never had a chance?)

My Zen teacher, Samu Sunim, says that people have to be miserable to discover Buddhism since it isn't advertised on any billboards and Buddhists don't go door to door selling magazines and enlightenment.

When I stumbled through the gate of the Zen Buddhist Temple for the first time I did not consider myself to be particularly miserable. It wasn't like I had cancer or I had lost a child to drugs. But I *did* have an eye twitch. And it wouldn't go away.

At the time, I was a highly paid management consultant working for an international firm, averaging seventy-hour work weeks in times of *non*crisis, of which there weren't many. As a strategy to market the firm, I had developed a series of entrepreneurial training programs, which I also ended up teaching myself since all my colleagues were completely busy with their own client work—when they weren't trying to actually spend some quality time at home attempting to remember their kids' names. As you can imagine, the eye twitch was incredibly distracting, a real nuisance. So I went to the eye doctor for a bandage that I could use to hold the twitch in place during seminars. Her response was to tell me that there was no such bandage, and that since the twitch was from stress, I could either a) get rid of the stress, or b) spend the rest of my life on Valium. I of course ignored her and took my eye twitch home, determined to ignore it. Which I was able to do until my other eye started twitching. Now, the problem with a double case of eye twitches is that the eyes don't twitch in sync, so focus becomes a memory. Of course, I needed to be able to drive my car and I also wanted to continue to see the people I was talking to. Call me old-fashioned.

I went back to the doctor. Again, she told me to get rid of the stress in my life. She even suggested that a meditation course might help. Having no idea what I was getting into, I picked up the phone book, looked up meditation courses, called the only number listed, signed up, and went. The twitch was gone in three weeks. *And* I discovered a whole new world, the world of Buddhism, a world I had no idea existed. The biggest shock of all was that it presented a world view that was consistent with all of my deepest beliefs. I learned that Buddhism embraces life's suffering as real, without denying its pain and heartaches. I learned that happiness is possible *if* we take responsibility for our own spiritual work and how we live each moment. I learned that we have faith in our own sincere hearts. (I can tell you now that your heart is sincere or you would not be reading this book.) I was relieved to hear early on that real spiritual work is hard work because we are responsible for our own progress. That made sense. It rang true.

I learned that the core tool of Buddhism is meditation, with its focus on the breath. We are taught to follow our breath, in and out, in and out, watching it leave us, watching it enter us. In the watching we are calmed, and are made ready for serious spiritual work. And while there are other tools—chanting, volunteering, prostrations (bowing to the floor)—it is meditation that forms the path we stumble on and the walking stick we can grasp when the going gets unbelievably rough. Meditation is what sneaks spiritual progress into our days, finally offering the taste of bliss that is at the bottom of all of our yearning.

Looking back, it amazes me that it took ten years of living in the same neighborhood to walk through the gate of the Ann Arbor Zen Buddhist Temple. During that time I was operating as a Unitarian, and there was, and still is, a part of me which was deeply wary of anything foreign to the culture I knew. That was the part that the eye twitch forced me to give up—the wary part. The curious part of me carried me through the gate. The curious part said out loud, "How hard could this be?"

How hard could this be? Following the meditation course, it took me a year of attending Sunday services to really find out. And it took a plunge into a retreat to formally start my stumbling on a spiritual path. Before that, outside of the miraculous healing of my eye twitch, my interest was purely intellectual, purely self congratulatory. I had tripped over a philosophy about living which proved that I knew what I had been talking about for some thirty-plus years. Retreats took me to a new level. My first was an overnight one. I loved it the way a kid loves swimming in a pond on a hot, sweaty summer day. I loved the quiet. When was the last time you were someplace that was really quiet? No television, no radio, no talking. The uninterrupted meditation sittings, each a half-hour long. The gentle words of encouragement by Reverend Sukha Linda Murray. The food: Completely healthy and surprisingly tasty to someone who had never even heard of half the dishes before. Miso soup, kimchee, steamed kale. The walking in the garden and in the meditation room. Even the manual work, which is a core component of the Buddhist spiritual path, was a wonderful exercise in learning how to do something just to do it. Since it was such a positive—almost sweet—experience, I decided to take a bigger bite and signed up for a five-day intensive retreat in Toronto, Canada. All this and living the life of a manic, harried, superficially happy management consultant. What a combination!

During the telling of the "good-old-days" stories that will always be a part of the Zen community in Ann Arbor, I had heard tales of all-night sittings, of chopping endless cords of wood to stay warm, of running barefoot in the snow, and even eating soup made solely of water, salt, and bean sprouts. I can remember packing for the worst before that first long retreat. Extra socks and extra layers of clothes. Ear plugs. Chocolate bars to stash in case that water, salt, and bean sprout soup ended up in front of me. A book in case it all got too scary. Midol, Tiger Balm, an extra pair of contact lenses in case one dried out from staring at the floor all day. Two kinds of scentless deodorant. An emergency address of a friend of a friend who lived nearby. I even left instructions with one relative to drive to Toronto to retrieve me if I wasn't back by ten o'clock on the day after the retreat ended. Though I never needed any of the items except the Midol for the headache I got from caffeine withdrawal, it was comforting to know that they shared my little sleeping space.

Samu Sunim's retreats always begin in the evening with words of encouragement and several sittings of meditation. A ten-minute break between sittings allows people to get some water, stretch a bit, and visit the bathroom. After every two sittings there is a walking (and occasionally jogging) meditation which lasts from fifteen to twenty minutes. This overall pattern starts at five-thirty every morning, following wake up and stretches, and continues until ten each evening. Following the last sitting of the day, participants are encouraged to continue their practice on their own—and most do, some through the night.

Each day provides time for manual work such as cleaning, stuffing meditation cushions, chopping wood, doing fix-up work on the temple grounds, or preparing meals. And there is at least one rest period each day. People who have never napped in their lives usually become rabid nappers by the second day's rest period. I was stunned when I discovered that I, a grown woman who had not napped since age two, could conk out in a room complete with outside traffic noise and radios blaring from the building next door, every time a rest period was offered.

Looking back over the years since I started participating in retreats, I find that they have become a collective memory lodged somewhere between my heart and brain. I do, however, have a strong sense of the waves of emotion I seemed to swim through each time I went. Excitement is always the overriding feeling at first. I am excited to be taking time off from whatever livelihood is mine and am eager for uninterrupted, concentrated spiritual time. Simultaneously, a nervousness plays hide-and-seek with me. Will I feel caged? Is this all some silly fantasy? Will I miss chocolate and/or sex so much that I can't think about anything else, blowing the whole retreat on a long line of obsessions? Will I get enough sleep? Will someone snore? Will I?

Day one is always a parade of catnaps. I can begin a retreat fully rested and still manage to sleep through most of the first day. And I always notice that I'm not alone. Our lives are taking a huge toll on us and, to a person, we are exhausted. Invariably, I find myself sitting on a cushion trying not to close my eyes, counting off minutes before the end of a meditation period, trying to hold on to my concentration, wondering what the heck ever possessed me to do this spiritual stuff in the first place, wondering if the Unitarians would have me back, eventually dozing. Then at last, at around eleven at night, sleep. Real dreamless sleep.

Phase two of a retreat usually starts in the middle of the second day. I call it my *whining-mind* phase, and I have been known to whine about every single thing that I can remember happening in my life that I have been unhappy about. Work. Kids. Husbands. Siblings. Crime. Violence. About my knees hurting and overpopulation. About my teacher. (Why couldn't he look just a little more like Richard Gere?) Whining about having to sit on the cushion and being furious that nobody ever warned me that this spiritual path stuff would be this hard. Wondering if I can take a lighter look at Catholicism. The whining can last a whole day, sometimes two, if I happen to be stuck in a difficult relationship or work environment.

Here is the miracle of retreats for me, and the reason why I have remained on this path, come hell or high water. *Because eventually the whining always stops.* I never know when it will stop. I just know that it does. Nor do I exactly understand why it does. I've somehow managed to realize that simply allowing the whining to just parade on through gives it the freedom to wind down...and then stop. Then there is just me and my spiritual practice. And then, after awhile, there is just the practice. Clear, clear practice. Just breathing. Just sitting. Just being. Everything is practice. And my heart explodes with love and gratitude and the deepest wish that every single person on the planet could taste this delicious taste, knowing that happiness is possible, real happiness. And if I can do it, you can too.

When people ask me where to start on this road to happiness I always hesitate, because there are many different legitimate spiritual paths to enlightenment. Perhaps as many ways as there are people. I happen to think Zen Buddhism is terrific because it is a straightforward and efficient form of spiritual practice. At its core is meditation. Meditation is our shovel, our walking stick, and our mother. Meditation is the main tool that we eventually use, with every breath we take. It can take a variety of forms. It can center around paying attention to each moment of our day. This is usually called "mindfulness meditation." Then there is "sitting meditation" where one follows one's breath, often concentrating on a sound, or a question that just doesn't seem to make sense such as, "What was your face before your mother was born?" This is perhaps the best known form of Buddhist meditation practice.

My teacher, Samu Sunim, instructs us that the very act of meditation is self-help because it is an expression of detachment and non-possession. When we sit in silence we come to accept ourselves just the way we are, and to be content with what we have:

> *"Truth, salvation, and enlightenment are not separate from oneself. You are the very source of what is true and wise. Buddhists say that all beings are Buddhas. That means that nothing originally is wrong with any of us. You have to trust yourself. You have to believe in yourself as a living embodiment of love and wisdom."*

The brilliance of meditation is that it is always available to each of us, wherever we are. With it you can always help yourself, no matter what happens to you and no matter how poorly you might feel about how you are living your life. No authority or power can override your own spiritual experience, your own spiritual awakening. And nothing can prevent you from helping yourself, unless you let yourself down. Over time you will realize that suffering really is optional. Once I had a sense of these truths I knew I was on my way. I knew I had a path to follow, and even if I stumbled a thousand times along the way, this was the path for me, because I was the one driving it and not someone else. And I could test its validity through my own experience. Because, when I finally learned to let go of having to totally control everything around me and let my life unfold, I was stunned by the results. How could I have ever thought I could outsmart the universe? That eye twitch gave

15

me what I needed to look around and do something about how I was living, what I was thinking, and ultimately what I believed. It led me back to trust, and hope, and belief.

Okay, I am getting maudlin here, and perhaps somewhat biased by my own experience. In the interest of a more even-handed fairness to all you emerging stumblers, I decided to take an unscientific survey of people drinking tea at the end of one of our Sunday services in Michigan to give you a feel for their experiences. A few are Buddhists. Most aren't. The question I asked was: How has meditation affected your life?

I have recorded their responses verbatim.

1. "I don't give people the finger as much when they cut me off on the highway."
2. "Me too."
3. "I don't tailgate as much."
4. "Me too." (Yes, this is the same person as #2)
5. "I've stopped trying to do so many things at the same time. I used to drive myself nuts..."
6. "I don't yell at my kids as much."
7. "I sexually fantasize all the time now." (Draw your own conclusions. The man wears short shorts to church.)
8. "I've forgiven my father."
9. "I've forgiven my mother."
10. "I haven't forgiven my father but I think I understand why he's like he is."
11. "It hasn't. This is my first time here."
12. "It hasn't. I keep falling asleep when I come here."
13. "I feel calmer."
14. "Me too." (Number 2 again.)
15. "Yeah, I feel calmer."
16. "What's this survey for anyway?"

Stumblers all. Welcome to our parade.

# Chapter Two

# First You Have to Row a Little Boat

---

*"It is like a boat going to the ocean. Before it reaches the ocean it is dragged with much effort, but once it reaches the ocean it is propelled without effort by the wind. The distance it travels on the ocean in one day is farther than it could be dragged by force in even a hundred years."*

—The Flower Ornament Scripture

---

Journal entry, July 5th: "We just ended a five-day summer retreat at ten yesterday morning. There were sixty of us. It was my best ever Zen warrior experience, given that the temperature hovered around 100 degrees F. I think I lost about seven pounds. Rain outside. The summer-smell fresh. The ducks are outside yapping for bread crumbs. Glad to be home. Very happy. Life is good."

It had been a retreat where we practiced intensively from five AM until after ten PM each day, the structure of the retreat protecting us (mostly) from our own wandering minds and desperate need to plan, control, direct. Chanting was our alarm clock. We rose quickly, and then, without showering or shaving or even eyeliner we each took a small bucket of soapy cold water and scrubbed our bodies clean. Once. Twice. Three times. We dressed quickly and ran downstairs and out of the building to jog or stretch or otherwise get our bodies moving, trying not to think of the rest of the neighborhood residents slowly waking up to coffee and CNN.

By five-thirty we were all lined up in the meditation hall to do one hundred and eight prostrations together. Walking up a mountain in one place is how I've heard it described. After the first set of twenty-five, a shout: "Great is the problem of birth and death!" The next twenty-five and a second shout: "Impermanence surrounds us!" Twenty-five more. "Be awake each moment!" And after the last batch of twenty-five: "Do not waste your life!" We do eight more. Our bodies are covered in sweat. I can taste salt in the hair locks that keep falling onto my face in spite of the series of braids I've made to keep my face clear of distractions. The breathing in the room is heavy. If someone was on the outside listening they would be sure they were hearing group sex.

Drenched, we sit for the first formal sitting of the day, beginning the pattern of sitting and resting, then sitting and walking. At the same time we take turns lining up for private interviews with Sunim. At the sound of a bell we run to him as fast as we know how. He offers encouragement. Sometimes its form is a shout, sometimes it is a whisper. Sometimes he just sits in practice with us. We return to the meditation hall encouraged, determined that this, this is the day of our enlightenment.

A formal lunch at one o'clock is followed by rest, then work, then more sitting. Then a snack and more sitting. Five days. We lose our sense of time, don't know if there has been a war, and remain fairly confident that the government is still standing and that nobody close to us has died. Our bodies teach us where we need some work, and somehow we all become more physically fit. Dharma spa. We learn that when we let go of our worries and our opinions what is left is pure practice, which is enlightenment. In Sunim's words we "get our own nostrils back" instead of continuing to be dragged around by something that is not really us. I listen to him and try not to laugh out loud. It is really hard. All I can picture is me with a big hoop in my nose that is tethered to a horse labeled "planning." It is dragging me all over the place, so much so that it lifts me right off the ground until I am this person-shaped flag trailing behind it. So much for enlightenment for this puppy, my mind thinks. I wonder: can we ever let go of our worries? Our opinions? They are such old friends. They have gotten us so far. They make us who we are, after all. The old timers can let go, some for an instant, some for longer. You can see it in their eyes. Shiny. Calm. Peaceful. Compassionate. And I know the old Zen masters have conquered their minds, but hey, this is the Nineties in the heartland of America. Get a grip. I'm busy wondering if I have lost enough weight to fit into my favorite little black dress again.

On day three, a shift. It's palpable. The whole group has jelled into a community. We seem to be breathing as one, moving as one. Sunim shouts at us, "Isn't it fun?" We can only laugh. Covered in sweat, sore from running and prostrations, we keep at it. Days pass, dissolving into a series of precious moments; our meditation filling us. Deeper and deeper we sink into the practice. The final day feels like we are floating in an emptiness which I can only describe as a soft joy.

I would walk a thousand miles to do it again.

It wasn't always so. It took years to dip my toe into this deep river that is a retreat, and even then I found excellent excuses not to stay at one for the whole time. My child was sick. I had deadlines. My mother was coming for a visit. I had important deadlines. My boyfriend just broke up with me. I had really big deadlines. A friend called from Australia and he might come to visit so I needed to stay home. I was in the middle of moving. It was the most important deadline of my professional career. The car broke down. I was wrong about the last deadline; THIS ONE IS THE ONE I NEED TO STAY HOME TO COMPLETE. (Impressed?) Finally, the simple momentum of my practice got me in the door and gave me the wherewithal to stay the heck put. Looking back, the decision to commit to a spiritual path came in tiny increments, starting with a whispered promise to myself, years ago, to just sit for five minutes to see what it was like.

Like all transformations, I have learned that stumbling toward enlightenment happens in fits and starts. And we all need to start at the beginning. It's like sailing. First you have to row a little boat. In his own reflection on life and living, *First You Row a Little Boat,* (Warner Books, 1993, pp. 7-14) Richard Bode tells a hilarious story of learning to sail.

Since it is so close to my own experience of learning how to meditate I decided to share my own "Cliffs Notes" version. As is true in any mastery, when you watch other people sail it always looks so easy. Smooth. If you are like me, or you are Richard, you assume that because it looks easy, well then, it is easy. This can get you into trouble fast. I see this often with people who come to the Zen temple and immediately throw themselves into our early morning sittings and monthly retreats only to leave in frustration, even anger, in a matter of months. They came for enlightenment, damn it, and they are furious that it hasn't happened. They assumed that they could sail a big boat without the training and the slow, slow build-up of concentration and faith that makes deep practice possible.

Back to Richard. "It seemed like such a simple sport. I thought all I had to do was raise the canvas, let it fill with wind, and the boat and I would take off together like a soaring bird." He would sit and watch a legendary skipper sail a charter boat in and out of bays and waterways with easy grace, obvious concentration, and a quiet endurance. My reaction to watching Sunim was the same. I would secretly stare at him whenever I was around him at first. His movements were effortless, his grace breathtaking, his concentration scary. Like Bode, I assumed that I would quickly become just like him, just like the master.

When Bode decides it's time to start sailing on his own he approaches an old sailor, asking him if he knows where there might be a boat for sale.

"Can you sail?"

"It was a question I dreaded, for one of the hardest things in life is to confess ignorance when trying to impress. I could deceive my friends—but the captain was a different matter. He was the master of an ancient art form I wanted to possess, and I knew he would see through my pretensions right away." Ditto.

Bode starts with a dinghy, a ten footer. In the same way we start sitting on the pillows from our beds or our couches. When Bode stepped onto the boat it almost pitched him into the water. When we first sit on our cushions our minds can't wait to start listing all the reasons why spending five minutes meditating is really really stupid. Or if we are living in a household with other people they will suddenly discover a hundred good reasons why they need our attention right now.

But Bode keeps going. "For three consecutive days I rowed that dinghy back and forth across the creek. Occasionally, the captain would walk out to the end of the dock, wave me ashore, and offer a few helpful hints, but most of the time he stood there quietly, watching....Hour by hour, day by day, under the captain's silent tutelage, I acquired a skill, which, as much as walking or talking, remains fundamental to my view of the world." Practice is the same. We need to start small. My own experience is that five minutes a day, every day, will carry us along just fine until something in us says "sit a little longer." As our bodies relax and our minds start to settle, our sitting naturally expands to six minutes, then seven, then ten, then twenty. Our practice, slowly, carefully, becomes who we are. And we become our practice. "And so in time the rowboat and I became one and the same—like the archer and his bow or the artist and his paint.

As our sittings improve we start to look for other ways to bring the rest of our lives in line with our meditation experience. I think I read at least twenty books on Buddhism in my first year. *Zen Mind, Beginners Mind*, anything I could find by Jack Kornfield, or Sharon Salzberg, or Thich Nhat Hanh. *The Dhammapada* over and over and over again. I wanted to know about the life of the Buddha. I wanted to know what happened to his relationships when he started turning his life over to his spiritual practice. What happened to his friendships? The news was not always good. And the more I read the more I understood that reading could never take the place of practice itself. It's like the difference between reading about great sex, and having great sex. Given the choice, which would you pick?

At first I had no idea how one lets all the various parts of a life come together in this realm. Then I tripped over the six paramitas, and the path started to take form.

## THE SIX PARAMITAS

- MAY I BE GENEROUS AND HELPFUL. (DANA)

- MAY I BE PURE AND VIRTUOUS. (SILA)

- MAY I BE PATIENT. MAY I BE ABLE TO BEAR AND FORBEAR THE WRONGS OF OTHERS. (KSANTI)

- MAY I BE STRENUOUS, ENERGETIC, AND PERSEVERING. (VIRYA)

- MAY I PRACTICE MEDITATION AND ATTAIN CONCENTRATION AND ONENESS TO SERVE ALL BEINGS. (DYHANA)

- MAY I GAIN WISDOM AND BE ABLE TO GIVE THE BENEFIT OF MY WISDOM TO OTHERS. (PRANA)

Ah. Guidelines. I could relax. I could do those things, I thought. Be generous and helpful. No sweat. Just don't ask to borrow my good coat. Helpful. Easy, as long as I'm not facing deadlines. Patience. Sure, sure, sure. I can wait a week or so for all of this good work to kick in. Energy is a definite yes, as long as there is a Starbucks within range. Meditation? If five minutes at a time is okay, I'm in. You can see how far back I started. Everything had to be MY RULES, with MY STRINGS attached. For awhile I carried around those paramitas like a golf score card, marking down screw-ups and giving myself points for when I had what I called a "Mother Theresa Day." It's a wonder I have any friends left, given the lack of Mother Theresa points earned.

Buddha also left clear ground rules for day-to-day living. More tools for my dharma toolbox. Precepts. In the *Digha Nikaya (Thus I Have Heard, The Long Discourses of the Buddha*, translated from the Pali by Maurice Walshe. Wisdom Publications, England, 1987, pp. 68-69), one of the collections of stories of the Buddha, the precepts show up in a wonderful story about a wandering teacher, Sappiya, who decides, along with his pupil Brahmadatta, that he is pretty mad about Buddha's growing positive reputation. So he starts to criticize him, only to hear his own pupil defend him. As you can imagine, this made Suppiya just furious. So he started following Buddha around, listening for things he could argue with. Over time he became increasingly brazen about criticizing Buddha, even to Buddha's own disciples.

They, in turn, got really angry and started to work up a real head of steam. The angrier they got, the noisier they were, until Buddha asked them what the heck was going on. When they told him about Suppiya's actions, his response was simply to shrug, instructing his followers that instead of getting angry, their job was simply to tell Suppiya that he was incorrect and let it go. To give them something else to think about, he then gave them a talk on morality and how to live their lives when they weren't busy meditating:

> "Abandoning the taking of life, the ascetic Gotama dwells refraining from taking life, without stick or sword, scrupulous, compassionate, trembling for the welfare of all living beings....
>
> Abandoning the taking of what is not given, the ascetic Gotama dwells refraining from false speech, a truth speaker, one to be relied on, trustworthy, dependable, not a deceiver of the world.
>
> Abandoning malicious speech, he does not repeat there what he has heard here to the detriment of these, or repeat here what he has heard to the detriment of those. Thus he is a reconciler of those at variance and an encourager of those at one, rejoicing in peace, loving it, delighting in it, one who speaks up for peace.
>
> Abandoning harsh speech, he refrains from it. He speaks whatever is blameless, pleasing to the ear, agreeable, reaching the heart, urbane, pleasing, and attractive to the multitude.
>
> Abandoning idle chatter, he speaks at the right time, what is correct and to the point, of Dhamma and Discipline."
>
> —(Digha Nikaya, p. 69)

For over a thousand years his words were passed along orally, generation to generation. With "modern" civilization and the short term memory loss that comes with stress, someone finally had the wisdom to put Buddha's words down on scrolls. Over time, such talks evolved into the Buddhist precepts, our very own rules of the road for living, guide-posts for indicating when we are on or off our spiritual path. Living according to the precepts, as with living with the ten commandments, helps our meditation to deepen—if only because we've screwed up slightly less than we did in our B.P. (before precepts) lives.

Happily, Thich Nhat Hanh, a well known Vietnamese monk, has created a user friendly version of the precepts, which can be found taped to any self-respecting Buddhist's refrigerator. They are:

1. Aware of the suffering caused by the destruction of life, I vow to cultivate compassion and learn ways to protect the lives of people, animals, and plants. I am determined not to kill, not to let others kill, and not to condone any act of killing in the world, in my thinking, and in my way of life.

2. Aware of the suffering caused by exploitation, social injustice, stealing, and oppression, I vow to cultivate loving kindness and learn ways to work for the well being of people, animals, and plants. I vow to practice generosity by sharing my time, energy, and material resources with those who are in real need. I am determined not to steal and not to possess anything that should belong to others. I will respect the property of others, but I will prevent others from profiting from human suffering or the suffering of other species on earth.

3. Aware of the suffering caused by sexual misconduct, I vow to cultivate responsibility and learn ways to protect the safety and integrity of individuals, couples, families, and society. I am determined not to engage in sexual relations without love and a long term commitment. To preserve the happiness of myself and others, I am determined to respect my commitments and the commitments of others. I will do everything in my power to protect children from sexual abuse and to prevent couples and families from being broken by sexual misconduct.

4. Aware of the suffering caused by unmindful speech and the inability to listen to others, I vow to cultivate loving speech and deep listening in order to bring joy and happiness to others and relieve others of their suffering. Knowing that words can create happiness or suffering, I vow to learn to speak truthfully, with words that inspire self confidence, joy, and hope. I am determined not to spread news that I do not know to be certain and not to criticize or condemn things of which I am not sure. I will refrain from uttering words that can cause division or discord, or that can cause the family or community to break. I will make all efforts to reconcile and resolve all conflicts, however small.

5. Aware of the suffering caused by unmindful consumption, I vow to cultivate good health, both physical and mental, for myself, my family, and my society by practicing mindful eating, drinking, and consuming. I vow to ingest only items that preserve peace, well being, and joy in my body, in my consciousness, and in the collective body and consciousness of my family and society. I am determined not to use alcohol or any other intoxicant or to ingest foods or other items that contain toxins, such as certain TV programs, magazines, books, films, and conversations. I am aware that to damage my body or my consciousness with these poisons is to betray my ancestors, my parents, my society, and future generations. I will work to transform violence, fear, anger, and confusion in myself and in society by practicing a diet for myself and for society. I understand that a proper diet is crucial for self-transformation and for the transformation of society."

(Reprinted from *For A Future To Be Possible: Commentaries on the Five Wonderful Precepts,* (1993) by Thich Nhat Hanh, with permission of Parallax Press, Berkeley, California.)

Whew. Seems like a lot. Too much for one person. I just read them for a long time. Then, yes I admit it, I taped them on the refrigerator, freeing my three-year-old collection of Sylvia cartoons. And I would stand in the kitchen sometimes, eating a bagel in the predawn morning, reading them, wondering if they would ever really penetrate my consciousness. Then, one day I found myself stopping for gas in a classic Midwestern "redneck" (not the Jeff Foxworthy, funny kind of redneck, the mean kind of redneck) town for gas. I know how redneck it is because I used to live there. There just happen to be an inordinately high level of card-carrying members of the Klu Klux Klan around those parts, a fact I never would have believed, if I hadn't experienced my own run-in with them some years earlier. Anyway, I got out of my car to pump gas. It was eight-thirty in the morning and pretty deserted. As I reached for the pump I noticed that all of a sudden eight pickup trucks were parked around me. It looked like every construction crew in a ten-mile radius had descended on the place for their first official coffee break of the day.

The second thing I noticed was a very large, as in well over six feet tall and two hundred pounds plus, young African American man making a call at the pay phone on the corner of the property. Here's the third thing I noticed. The pickup guys were watching his every move. Like cats. Really watching. Remember a time when you could feel someone watching every little thing you were doing even though your back was to them—that kind of watching. There were at least six sets of eyes watching him make his phone call. *Dana Paramita. May I be kind and generous.* Of all the thoughts that could have surfaced. I was amazed. So, I casually walked up to the young man who, as I got closer, looked bigger and bigger and younger and younger, and asked him if he could use a ride somewhere. He said he could. His truck had broken down on the highway and he was thirty-five miles from where he lived. I drove him home. Maybe I saved his life. Maybe I'm just paranoid. What I do know is that without the combination of my meditation practice and the constant reading of the precepts during my stand-up meals, I might not have noticed him and even if I had, I would never, as a small woman, have had the courage to walk up to a young man more than twice my size, to offer him a ride.

# Chapter Three

# More Tools for Your Spiritual Toolbox

---

## THE EIGHTFOLD PATH

| | | |
|---|---|---|
| *Right Speech* | *Right Action* | *Right Livelihood* |
| *Right Effort* | *Right Awareness* | *Right Thought* |
| *Right Concentration* | ◆ | *Right Understanding* |

---

As we stumble toward enlightenment some part of us becomes hungrier and hungrier for more guidelines. Buddha, of course, was ready for this. His most famous teachings in this regard became known as the Noble Eightfold Path. It consists of three parts or stages. *Shila,* or moral practice, is the first. Moral practice has to do with steering clear of immoral or unwholesome speech or behavior. The second stage is *samadhi* or the practice of concentration, which in turn gives us the ability to have some control over our own mental processes (on our good days). With *shila* and *samadhi* comes wisdom, or *prajna*. Think of *prajna* as those occasional insights that make your life run smoother, your days happier. The three stages are further defined by eight steps: right speech, right action, right livelihood, right effort, right awareness, right concentration, right thought, and right understanding.

The first three steps have to do with our manifested behavior, how we talk, what we talk about, what we do, how we earn our living. In a perfect world we would all have complete and compassionate conscious control over our words and deeds so we would never harm anyone or anything. But it's not a perfect world and we make mistakes. And who among us is completely conscious anyway? Not me. That's for certain.

Knowing that this is our regular state, semiconscious at best, trying, but stumbling, Buddha suggested that by simply practicing kind and wholesome speech and actions we would not only evolve spiritually, we would be much happier as we go. Works for me. To be able to meditate well, our minds need to be calm and quiet. How can they be if we have just yelled at someone, or been yelled at, slammed the door, made the nasty phone call, kicked the dog? We can't. In my case, meditation is hopeless if I have just finished listing all the reasons why I am the only person who is right in my universe, or been cut off in traffic, or my daughter has just reminded me that I am completely without fashion sense so would I please stop trying. Sit calmly? Not a chance. As S. N. Goenka says in *Entering the Stream: An Introduction to the Buddha and His Teachings,* "Whenever one commits unwholesome action, the mind is inundated with agitation. When one abstains from all unwholesome actions of body or speech, only then does the mind have the opportunity to become peaceful enough so introspection may proceed....One who practices is working toward the ultimate goal of liberation from all suffering. While performing this task he cannot be involved in actions that will reinforce the very mental habits he seeks to eradicate. Any action that harms others is necessarily caused and accompanied by craving, aversion, and ignorance." (*Entering the Stream: An Introduction to the Buddha and His Teachings,* edited by Samuel Bercholz and Sherab Chodzin Kohn, Shambala, Boston, 1993, p.98) Committing such actions is taking two steps back for every step forward, thereby thwarting our progress.

What is unwholesome speech? Like pornography, you know it when you hear it. Telling lies, spreading rumors, backbiting (that favorite American pastime), swearing, making insults, dissing, and even idle chit-chat which has no usefulness, are all examples of unwholesome speech. They agitate the mind, forcing us to lose our focus. We stumble. *Right speech* is kind, quiet, happy. It is compassionate. It lifts us, gives us energy, steadies our step.

For *right action*, there are some obvious things we don't want to do like killing, stealing, rape, adultery, or the seduction of inappropriate partners, or getting so drunk or high that we have no idea what we are doing, or even if we do know we've lost the ability to control ourselves, or even care. These things do not constitute right action. Instead, we want to harm as little as possible, cherishing everything, aware of how precious it all is.

*Right livelihood* is vital because most of our adult lives circle this issue of how to labor for pay in a way that does not harm the earth or each other. It's tougher than it sounds. At its most basic level, living a *right livelihood* life means earning wages without breaking the precepts. Remember those? No killing, stealing, lying, etc. And it counts against us if we encourage other people to break the precepts. Harm is harm.

It doesn't take a huge amount of thinking to determine where we won't be spending our time on this path. As we play out the consequences of our work on our own lives and the lives of others, we can see the impact this has. For example, a gambling casino may not obviously break the precepts, but anyone who has spent time in one can see the harm it causes to the people there. The point of course is to pay attention to our decisions, to think them through as best we can before we make them.

Here's another example. The community I live in is chock full of nonprofit groups. One of my favorites is a local art association. Recently a close friend of mine told me they were looking for help with a strategic plan, something I love to do when I am not writing, needing to be right, or working hard at my own personal version of the ministry. At first blush it was an obvious match. Thinking more deeply I remembered that one of the organization's single largest sources of income is a masterful wine auction for which they have become quite well known. I deal with the effects of alcoholism every day. My father is one. So are many of the people I spend my time with. You may be. After all, it's more than twenty percent of us. I've seen lives lost, children abused, and whole families bankrupted by alcohol. I didn't make the phone call. Buddha wasn't stupid. Those precepts are literal.

The next three steps of the Eightfold Path help us learn how to better concentrate our minds so we can truly sail these little meditation boats, our bodies. *Right effort* has to do with giving our spiritual practice our best shot, over and over and over, however many times we need to climb back on the path. It teaches us how to focus our minds, not an easy task for a society which takes great pride in doing more than one thing at a time. I just squirm now when I remember how proud I used to be when I was able to carry on a business telephone conversation while jogging in place and opening my mail—sometimes even entertaining my young daughter if she happened to be in the room.

> *"Who is in control here? As soon as one begins....it becomes very clear very quickly that in fact the mind is out of control. Like a spoiled child who reaches for one toy, becomes bored, and reaches for another, and then another, the mind keeps jumping from one thought, one object of attention to another, running away from reality."* — (S. N. Goenka, p. 103)

So we screw up. We start again; we fail; we start again. Sometimes concentration stays with us a little longer. When we are distracted we pause and start all over again. We're the little boat that can sail, the little engine that could—however many lifetimes it takes. *Right awareness* comes in here. Once I started to be able to watch my thoughts I discovered that my thinking was a combination of planning, worrying, and laughing, with a liberal salting of sexual fantasy. While there is no inherent problem with any of these, what it did mean is that most of the time I was not even living my own life. When I was lost in yearning or planning or remembering, I wasn't aware of what was going on in that moment. When I was lost in a different time warp, I was condemned to the same mental treadmill that had brought me to the temple door in the first place, a treadmill which, while entertaining, had not led to any real happiness.

Spiritual practice is about here and now—that's the road we're traveling. To be right here, right now, we need to learn how to pay attention, and as our attention and awareness expand, a miracle happens: The planning slows down, the worries decrease, sexual fantasies taper off. We stumble less often. However tiny a moment of right awareness, its experience can keep us going because it is our very own proof that we don't have to be slaves of our ego minds.

I discovered that when we can hold onto our awareness, *right concentration* becomes possible. Over time, concentration brings with it a deep sense of relaxation and energy. Our minds become peaceful and our breath soft. Concentration becomes our weapon against thoughts of fear, worry, and panic. Not that concentration is everything. It can't weed out the roots of our cravings all by itself, our need for a beer, or a sexual partner. But it is an excellent start.

If Buddha had stopped at six, his Sixfold Path would have reflected the teachings of the other world religions to lead a moral life and to pray. But Buddha went for extra credit. Based on his own experience he realized that the six steps would only get us so far. Wrapped up in them I can be furious about something, and sit in meditation until it's gone. But when I stop meditating my anger returns. So step seven goes after roots. *Right thought.* Right thought is about trading in old negative thoughts for positive ones. "I am so stupid" is traded for "I gave it my best shot." "She's so stupid" is traded in for "she's doing the best she knows how." It's like adulterous love affairs. Very deep damage comes out of adultery. A person is in a committed relationship, yet somehow she takes a wrong turn, and ends up in bed with someone who isn't her marriage partner. Now, I have never, ever, known anyone to wake up one morning and say, "Hmm. Today is a good day to go out and meet someone with whom I can have an affair." No one consciously intends it. And often the people who have the affair are as hurt and scared as everyone around them once the dust settles. Understanding where the behavior came from, what its roots are, can be far more valuable for healing than needing to judge the behavior. *Right thought* is about letting go of that need to judge so we can really gain an understanding of what the heck our lives are really all about. We let go of our addiction to judging everyone and everything, and trade it in for a simple quest for understanding.

*Right thought.* I started to understand how other people's opinions were leading me around like a bull with a ring through its nose. I started to understand how, whatever anyone else thought—positive or negative—what mattered was whether or not I was offering each situation "the best me" available. That was enough.

Over time, such *right thinking* leads to the last step of the Eightfold Path, *right understanding,* or real wisdom. I admit that *right understanding* can be a real rush. It's insight heaven. A wonderful feeling comes with simply understanding the dynamics of a situation from a perspective that is not driven by ego. We see truth—moment to moment truth—and with that comes the understanding that life will give us each about a gazzilion chances to flex our spiritual understanding muscles, or enough groundhog days to keep us wildly entertained our whole lives. Our wisdom grows out of our own experience, as does our growing spiritual self. This is the proof of the usefulness of Buddhism; this is the ocean that we can now sail.

So we have the tools: the precepts, the paramitas, the Eightfold Path. As we stumble along with these goodies in our mental knapsack, can anything get in our way? Does anything? The short answer—everything gets in our way at first. We're like these sensory craving addicts who are trying desperately to stay straight but we keep tripping up, straying into our pasts, fast-forwarding into our futures. We love, love, love our egos. And why not? They have been with us for as long as we can remember.

The thing is that some part of us knows that our ego life hasn't been truly happy. There have been a few good moments, but how many orgasms can you have in a day really? So we start meditating; we stop; we sail; we stumble. We go back to drinking or we call an old lover. But now there is this little voice that knows better and won't leave us alone. So each time we go back to ego, our visit is a little shorter. We go back to our practice—trip back onto the path, patiently and persistently, because if we can run a 10K race, then we can sit here and meditate for ten minutes. If we can meet deadlines, pay the bills, make the marriage proposal, keep the dog away from the neighbor's cat, then we can meditate before bed.

What are the benefits of all this practice, of using these tools, of starting over and over and over? There are many. First of all, it may just save your life. It may give you the courage to get out of a toxic situation that your heart knows is killing you slowly but surely. It may simply melt away negative emotions. You may discover that, over time, you are more relaxed with your life. You may simplify your days by weeding out the gunk, such as letting go of that love affair that really ended back in 1987. (Who cares who he's with now???!!! You have a life to live and time is precious.) Flashes of happiness may occur. Your energy increases and, for most people, a subtle layer of peacefulness and joy starts to form, sort of like that bacteria we grew on agar back in high school biology class.

So become one with *your* practice, your Eightfold Path. Embrace it as though it was the lover you have waited for all your life. Ride with it, swim with it, sink with it, soar with it. Sail and sail hard. I'll go with you. Enlightenment is waiting for us on the other side of the ocean. And it will wait for however long it takes.

# Chapter Four

# Mind Games

---

*"We are what we think.*
*All that we are arises with our thoughts.*
*With our thoughts we make the world.*
*Speak or act with a pure mind*
*And happiness will follow you*
*As your shadow, unshakable."*

—The Dhammapada

---

*We are what we think.* If nothing else, affirmations have taught us this truth. When I read an affirmation that says, "Today is a perfect day for feeling love for your friends and family," I can literally sense a feeling of love and appreciation surface in my consciousness. I'd probably be a great candidate for hypnosis. *We are what we think.* If someone says something that we think is just wrong or stupid, we can suddenly find ourselves "better than them," somehow on a higher plane. *We are what we think.* If the medical community has taught us anything in recent years, it is how intimately connected our health is to what is going on in our minds. If we are consumed with worry and anxiety—which is true for many of us—heart disease, immune system breakdowns, and other physical problems can surface as a result.

*We are what we think.* I just love it when someone in the business world adds input into the world of spiritual stumblers. Peter Senge, whose name you may recognize, is a management consultant, some would say guru, who has spent years introducing a collection of teachings called *The Fifth Discipline* into corporate America. He must be hitting a chord because he has been invited into a wide variety of companies of all types and sizes, from Shell Oil to Harley-Davidson to Hanover Insurance, to the Ford Motor Company. One of his five disciplines is learning how to surface our own mental models. In other words, he teaches people how to see what they are thinking. We all have mental models. I'm sure that Senge has a formal corporate definition for them. Mine is this: We are, each of us, walking around with deeply held beliefs of how the world, and everything in it, works. It's how we stay sane, assuming we are. It's how we fit everything that happens to us together into a world view that makes sense to us. Mental models are our images, our assumptions about all that we encounter, the stories we believe to be true. One of the all-time best examples of mental models hard at work is the emperor in the story, *The Emperor's New Clothes.* Even though the man is butt naked, he is convinced he is wearing a suit of exquisite clothing. In the same way I am dead certain that I am, indeed, a fashion princess, even though my thirteen-year-old flatly refuses to be seen anywhere with me in public, including the grocery store. I think it's because I fold my socks, or maybe the denim in my jeans is too light. Maybe it's everything. She has her own mental models, and one is that it is virtually impossible for a mother to have fashion sense.

Adding to Senge, Chris Argyris, a professor at Harvard, says that we are utterly true to our mental models. *We are what we think.* So if we believe that people are untrustworthy, we will treat everyone as though they can't be trusted, even those who would protect us with their lives, give us the shirt off their back, their last piece of pizza, the foot massage we have been thinking about for weeks. Like most parents, I happen to believe that my daughter is incredibly smart, maybe a genius. As a result I am always disappointed when she walks in the door with a report card full of "Bs," even when I have been told by her teachers that she did her best. My mental model is that a smart teen should get "As." All of my disappointment is directly related to my own mental models, my own thoughts, and may have nothing at all to do with the level of her effort.

Consider the damage done by societal mental models which often manifest as unfounded prejudice. What are the mental models behind the religious wars still being waged in many parts of the world, or the family feuds that last lifetimes and then some? So many of our mental models have little relation to reality. Think of all of the relationships that you know of that crumbled because one person expected the other to take care of them (even though nothing was ever said), or where one thought the other would at least always be home to cook dinner.

The damage is deep because our thoughts, our mental models, literally affect what we see. You and I can see exactly the same event and describe it in utterly different ways, as eyewitness accounts to automobile accidents have proved. A party which I remember as the dullest, most boring nonevent is your favorite event of the past twenty years because the people involved weren't all in hyper speed mode and were relaxed for once in their adult lives.

One of the most fun experiments I have ever participated in was a business retreat where a bunch of us were shown a picture of an office on a big screen for a couple of seconds and were then given instructions to list what we had seen. Like the well-trained students that we were, we wrote lists and lists of things—chairs, desks, note pads, clocks, computers, rugs. Not one of us noticed the toaster oven on the desk, or the food blender, or the toilet brush. But we all saw chairs which weren't even in the picture, and the clock on the wall which wasn't there either. One of us caught the little stove in the corner but couldn't quite tell what it was. Mouse pads on a work station?

The thing about mental models is that they seem to grow and harden like concrete until we are convinced that our beliefs are THE TRUTH and based on real data. Here is an example from the Senge team: "For example I am standing before the executive team, making a presentation. They all seem engaged and alert, except for Larry, at the end of the table, who seems bored out of his mind. He turns his dark, morose eyes away from me and puts his hand to his mouth. He doesn't ask any questions until I'm almost done, when he breaks in: 'I think we should ask for a full report.' In this culture that typically means, 'Let's move on.' Everyone starts to shuffle their papers and puts their notes away. Larry obviously thinks I'm incompetent, which is a shame, because these ideas are exactly what his department needs. Now that I think of it, he's never liked my ideas. Clearly, Larry is a power hungry jerk. By the time I've returned to my seat, I've made a decision: I'm not going to include anything in my report that Larry can use. He wouldn't read it or, worse still, he'd just use it against me. It's too bad I have an enemy who's so prominent in the company." (*The Fifth Discipline Fieldbook: Strategies and Tools for Building a Learning Organization*, by Peter Senge, Art Kleiner, Charlotte Roberts, Richard B. Ross, Bryan J. Smith. Currency Doubleday, New York, New York, 1994, pp. 242-243)

Who knows what Larry was thinking. Maybe he just found out he has prostate cancer. Maybe his partner just left him. Maybe someone gave him the finger while he was driving to work. Maybe he's just tired, or maybe, just maybe, he didn't have anything to say because the speaker did a good job. We can be so deluded and here's the corner we get ourselves in: Delusion builds on itself and evolves into a chain reaction that people like Senge call a ladder of inference. It's amazing. What happens is that you or I might see or hear or smell or taste something. So far so good. But then we "select" data based on our own belief structure or world view. In other words, our mental models kick in. Then we add meaning to it (the guy is a jerk) and make even more assumptions about the situation based on those meanings. Before we know it, these assumptions have led to conclusions (he'll never help me) which lead to a whole belief structure (I have an enemy and it is Larry) which drives future actions (I wouldn't help that creep if he was the last person on earth).

We all do it. I remember ending a relationship with someone I really cared about just because he never showed up on time. I took the data—being late—and translated it into his not caring about me, which then transformed into his never being there for me, and finally into needing to end the relationship before I got hurt badly. It didn't matter that he was kind, generous, honest, compassionate, and smart. He was always late and that was that. Of course I don't need to tell you that for ten years now he has been happily married to a woman who didn't share my delusions.

What's so painful is that we are typically so caught up in our unending stream of mental modeling that we rarely take the time to stop and question ourselves. So we live lives clouded by misunderstandings, communication breakdowns, anger, and violence. Even if we don't slug someone, we'll do something self-destructive like grind our teeth down to nothing with all the tension created.

How do we put on the brakes? We watch our thinking, reflect on it and make it visible, including our reasoning. We ask others how they got to their conclusions so we are exposed to alternative reasoning.

Buddhism often addresses the purgatory of mental models. Bundled together they add to delusion, which Buddhist writers write about, Buddhist teachers talk about, and Buddhist practitioners wrestle with constantly.

Delusion is about deception, even madness. When we are totally deluded we are totally wrong about a given situation—believing in unreality. Here's my favorite delusion in our society: that there are "second class" citizens. Are we all born with invisible tattoos that categorize us all like different cuts of meat? I keep looking for my tattoo; especially in situations where I get the distinct feeling that someone has labeled me in some way. Before you get too smug thinking that you aren't a member of our "Deluded People's Club," try watching your own immediate reaction to all of the people you come into contact with this week. All I know is that I am treated very differently by the world, familiar faces included, depending on what I'm wearing, not to mention hairstyle. There's the dressed-in-a-speech-making-appropriate-tailor-made-business-suit response. There's the short-hair-plus-gray-monk's-robes response. There's the tee-shirt-sweats-and-sneakers response. There's the just-plain-grungy, haven't-taken-a-shower-and-no-I-don't-shave-my-legs response. The same person, same IQ, same color, same weight (mostly), same sex, same age. And I get totally different reactions. It's as though we all have television channels in our heads and as we live our lives we tune in to a particular channel, seeing exactly what we look for, whether it's there or not. As a result, if you are primarily preoccupied or tuned to the physical body, as you look at people you see them as man or woman, fat or thin, tall or short, attractive or unattractive. If on the other hand, you think a lot about psychology, you might see the same people as introverted or extroverted, happy or sad. It's all in the eyes of the beholder.

So here we are, *being what we think.* We are deluded by our consciousness, which is attached to our senses, or our antennae. And we get into such trouble when we take this world of appearances for a whole reality. To top it off, we often then translate appearance into meaning, believing that the world is outside of us (that there is a subject-object split).

Talk about a mess.

Consider this, just consider this: NOTHING IS OBJECTIVE in a mental-model world. Even when we work hard to perceive something with all of our senses we aren't getting the whole hit.

Sincere spiritual practice, whatever its form, can weaken our deluded state. The *Heart Sutra,* which is sort of a summary of Buddhist teachings that is chanted throughout the world, teaches us this. In the sutra, a great teacher, Avalokiteshvara, teaches us that form is emptiness and emptiness is form. In the same way, feeling, thought, impulse, and consciousness are also empty. They are nothing by themselves. Whenever there is self, whenever there is ego, there is delusion. And piles upon piles of mental models, which make letting go of delusion harder than anything, harder than giving up our favorite mind-spinning drug, whether its sex, drugs, alcohol, power, or busyness.

Yet we must let go because our stumbling toward enlightenment depends on it. It is in our meditation, our silences, in the slowing down of our lives where we learn about delusion, and about letting go. Here is an example of what I mean. When I pick up a piece of paper what I see is paper, a thing, and at first, a separate thing. Depending on its shape, size, color, and texture, it may be pleasant (an invitation to a masked ball) or unpleasant (a letter from the Internal Revenue Service telling me I owe them more money than I have). Through my spiritual practice I realize that paper isn't paper; it's the divine. It's the sun that grew the tree that was turned into paper. It's the rain that fed the tree. It's the tree. It's the logger who felled the tree, and the person who raised him so he could. It's the printer and the paper maker and their parents and their parents' parents. It's the material that went into the printing press, and lots, lots more.

The point is that *everything* is completely and utterly interconnected. You and me, and all of the people we have ever known, and all the sunrises and sunsets, and the farms, and snow, and school bus drivers, and employers, and bankers, everyone who got us this far. How can we feel separate? How can we judge each other and how can we waste our precious time even trying to? I cringe when I think of all the time I spend judging. Can you name one thing that isn't connected to other things? Even a cloud was water before it was a cloud. Maybe it was a river, or maybe tears. The tree outside your window grew from someone's ashes, maybe another tree's, surely some animals and insects, maybe someone's great-great-grandfather. As far as I can tell even the quantum scientists are with me on this. Nothing is created and nothing is destroyed. Even the best scientist on the planet is incapable of reducing the smallest element to nothingness. One form of energy can only become another form of energy. Please try to understand this, to penetrate it with all your will and concentration because it is the window to understanding.

So let's flush out those mental models we're carting around. They can usually be found just under the surface of our awareness. Meditation helps us to learn how to watch our thoughts and see the patterns in them. We discover what we think is good, and why, and what we call better, or worse. We learn who we truly admire and who we don't, and even review, sort of like a life review, all the biases we've ever had—while sitting in silence on a cushion. This can be an absolutely amazing experience, a teaching of a lifetime. Meditation offers the opportunity to focus on a mental model or delusion from different vantage points, instead of being our normal reactive selves. Rooted quietly in a state of awareness, we have this space which lets us "watch" our reactions, understanding them in a much broader context than a single situation or series of situations. Clarity comes, and with it, over time, comes wisdom and compassion—the two sides of spiritual progress. We discover that we really do carry heaven and hell with us. Our practice alerts us to which side is winning us over moment by moment.

I never realized how much I judge people—particularly when it comes to appearance—until I started this stumbling thing. I clearly remember one of my first silent retreats when I had a read on every single person who was there by the end of the first break. I knew who I liked and who I didn't like (thin, pretty blond women were my least favorite since they made me feel fat, unattractive, and gray in comparison). All this, without a single word spoken. I knew who had money, who didn't, who would be my friends, who wouldn't, who my next lover would be—the curly-haired, tall man in the corner. When we were finally able to actually meet each other and talk at the end of the retreat I had to laugh out loud at my totally deluded state. The prettiest young blond woman was wise, warm, and witty, filled with compassion, and a Catholic nun! The curly-haired tall man has absolutely no interest in women. The old guy who drove us all nuts with his fidgeting and noisy breathing is a famous theater director. So much for my silent conclusions. I learned that you really can't judge a book, or a person, by its cover.

And that's the point, and the lesson. Never think that you know. Let's work it into our days.

# Chapter Five

# A Buddhist Approach to Anger

*"Let go of anger.*
*Let go of pride.*
*When you are bound by nothing*
*You go beyond sorrow."*
—The Dhammapada

Wow, are we ever angry. We're angry at the politicians and they're all angry at each other. We're angry at virtually all institutions. Men are angry at women. Women are still angry at men. Kids are angry at their parents and parents are angry at the teachers, who are angry back. Even our pets are suffering; depression among dogs is at an all-time high. If it wasn't so painful we might all be characters in a Dr. Seuss book. I'd be in the one about the sneetches or maybe *The Butter Battle Book.*

But anger is painful. When it is expressed outwardly it can become verbally and physically violent, leading to spouse abuse, child abuse, stranger abuse, eventually even war. If it moves inward it leads to depression, obsessions, despair, and increasingly, suicide. Which doesn't even begin to describe the damage anger does to our bodies: heart attacks, nervous diseases, ulcers, cancer. While it may be true that anger can be useful when it creates the energy to get out of a dangerous situation, this form of anger seems to be the rare exception these days.

What can we do? When I was growing up I was taught to fight anger with anger. If the kid hit you, the correct response was to hit him back. That can be a real problem if you are the spunkiest kid in the schoolyard—the one with the smart mouth—the one the class bully likes to pick on the most because he can knock you down with one blow. I tried hitting back, true to my training. I lost two teeth the first time. When I tried it again, he broke my arm. Finally I decided to get my two little sisters to help (together we added up to his weight). He beat them up too. Happily we moved right about then, but not before I learned that a return of anger just escalates the fire. It doesn't solve anything; not in my childhood and not now.

There's another attitude toward anger many of us take: "Just forget about it." If only it worked. First of all, when we're angry we're often angry for legitimate reasons. The politician is corrupt. It was sexual abuse. My mate is having an affair. My son is cheating in school. "Forgetting about it" is like pretending that the emperor has clothes on. It is ignoring the elephant in the room. It is classic denial and quite literally eats at our gut.

Buddhism offers another approach. A big chunk of Buddhist teachings is about the psychology of living sane lives. It's not just about mental models but about much, much more. Lives where peace and compassion are possible. In other words, there is a 2,500-year-old tradition of figuring out techniques for transforming our angry minds into peaceful minds—not passive—peaceful.

But first a story. Years ago, before any of us were around, there were two brothers who lived on top of a mountain in their own little monastery. The older brother was known throughout the land as the best debater in the entire country. Nobody could beat him in an argument. Nobody. The younger brother had never tried his hand at debating because he had lost one of his eyes as a child and was so self-conscious about it that he had kept himself hidden so nobody would see him. One day when they were upstairs in their kitchen they heard a knock on their downstairs door and suddenly a shout: "I'm here to debate!" The older brother just groaned and said to his younger brother, "Look, I've been the one doing the debating all these years...it's your turn for a change." At first the younger brother refused, but then he looked out the window and saw that it was just a teenage boy outside so he decided to give it a try and down the stairs he went. Within minutes the teenager came running up the stairs with a big grin on his face, bowed to the older monk and exclaimed, "No wonder you brothers have such an excellent reputation! I bowed to your brother and held up one finger to say that Buddha is a great teacher. So he bowed back and held up two fingers to mean that Buddha and his teachings are our guides. Then I held up three fingers to say that Buddha, his teachings, and our community are what make life worthwhile. At that point your brother lifted his fist and shook it, meaning, 'It's really all the same in the end, isn't it?' Brilliant! Brilliant!" and out the door he ran. Seconds later the younger brother came up the stairs shouting, "Where is that bastard?! I'm going to punch him in the face...." His brother stopped him and asked what happened. "Well," the younger brother replied, "We bowed and the first thing I knew he held up one finger meaning, 'How's it going one-eye?' I chose to ignore his rudeness and bowed and held up two fingers meaning, 'It is wonderful to meet you, young monk with two eyes.' At which point the rascal bowed and held up three fingers to say, 'Yes, but we still only have three eyes between us.' Just as I raised my fist to hit him he ran from the room."

Our emotions combined with our mental models define the situation. This is *always* true. When we pay attention, particularly to the emotions we bring into a situation, we see how easily we take a neutral, or even potentially positive situation, and transform it into anger-producing moments. Here's a more recent example: One Sunday two friends of mine offered to take me to lunch in downtown Chicago. At a stoplight on the way to a diner, a man crossed the street directly in front of us. He looked just like Groucho Marx—the nose, the eyebrows, the glasses, the mustache. They were all there. Delighted, I pointed him out exclaiming, "The real Groucho. How wonderful!" At which point he stopped right in front of the car, wiggled his mustache and gave me the finger. My friends said I was lucky he didn't have a gun. He assumed my delight and appreciation was ridicule and had needlessly responded with anger.

Now, I don't learn lessons easily. On the way back from lunch (I'm sure these people will never ask me to lunch again) we were driving through a busy side street when a teenage boy rounded a corner and, without missing a beat, picked an empty coffee container out of a garbage can and started panhandling. He was beautiful. Army punk clothes. Hair divided into three triangles each about a foot long. The top one was rose colored, the color of a deep sunset. Silver jewelry covered his arms and he had several sets of earrings on his face.

I was enthralled. I just couldn't get enough of him. His skin was a deep olive color, eyes a dark chocolate brown, his grin wider than the sky. He caught me smiling at him. Giving me one finger wasn't enough. He set the coffee cup down so he could use both hands! There it was again. Instant anger. It seems to be everywhere. And all it seems to take to trigger it is a wrong word or look.

What can we do? I propose a four-step process which comes out of both the Tibetan and Zen traditions. The steps are, first to *be gentle with yourself*. Second, allow yourself to feel the anger so you can see what the real emotion is behind it. Third is learning to empathize with the other (this is not the same thing as accepting their behavior). And finally, there is the need for patience. If a fire isn't fed, it burns out. The same is true for anger.

Now for the details. In order to first loosen the grip of anger we need to be gentle with ourselves, to let ourselves make mistakes because that is what life is all about—making mistakes so we can learn from them. Being gentle with yourself means giving yourself enough sleep so you aren't walking around in a sea of fatigue, so tired that you overreact at the first sound you don't like. Being gentle with yourself means eating healthy, filling food so your body doesn't growl at every-thing that strikes you the wrong way. It means protecting yourself from the unnecessary violence that comes in the form of television shows (have you watched any cartoons lately?), movies, and newspapers.

Being gentle with yourself means saying something once and then letting it go. Or reminding someone who feels a compulsion to correct you in some way that you heard them the first time and don't need a replay.

It means ridding yourself of negative self-talk. I had no idea how often I said to myself, "You can do better than that," until I started to pay better attention to my own thoughts. Slowly, "Good try" has become the substitute thought. Being gentle means finding time to relax, play, walk rather than run, and watch an entire movie at home without getting up once to do a chore.

The process of opening up your heart, first to yourself, allows you to start to see situations AS THEY ARE, instead of viewing them through the mirror of your emotions, not to mention those old friends, your mental models. Plus your body will thank you. From the compassion that grows out of the gentleness you will be able to undertake the next steps.

The second step is the scariest. It is to just *feel the anger*. In Buddhism we tell ourselves to sit on the cushion and face the tiger right then and there. The Tibetan saint Milarepa was sort of an early version of Superman, able to leap tall mountains in a single bound, and stuff like that. What he discovered was that all those super athletic accomplishments didn't get rid of his fears and negative emotions; they just put them off. Whenever he went home to his cave for a rest his demons would always be there waiting for him. Finally he decided to simply sit with them and wait them out. Slowly but surely they all went away. Except one. Fear. He stared at it for awhile and finally told it to open its mouth so he could climb inside. At that, it dissipated. He faced his "dragon" and won.

We all have our dragons. For most of us, sitting with anger leads us to the real emotions behind it. Sometimes we find hurt. Most often it's fear. I say stare it down. Feel it. Feel it until you start to see its humor, or you're bored, or you have just plain had enough. Sit with it until then. This won't take as long as you think, and the anger really will go away.

Sometimes people tell me they're afraid they'll go crazy if they let themselves feel their anger. My response has always been, "Why do you think you aren't crazy now? Anger makes you crazy." You can't think clearly. Feel. Talk. Function. Your dragon is winning, and it will continue to win until you show it who is boss—the you that is inherently wise, good, and kind; the you who doesn't need to be angry to know what to do in a given situation. What most of us find, in fact, is that it is our resistance to anger, or a denial of anger, that causes the most pain, much more than the anger itself.

About two years ago I had a full-fledged panic attack. I had heard about them from some friends and had also read about them, but I had somehow relegated them to manifestations of high anxiety—not an everyday experience certainly, but nothing to change your life. Then I had one. Me, a woman who skis double black diamond trails, sky dives, surfs ten-foot waves, and meditates in caves with bats, had a panic attack over taking my daughter to the hospital for a skin cancer test. I was on the floor. When I was finally able to get up, brush myself off, and begin to function, I went to a therapist for advice. To my surprise and delight she suggested that the next time it happened I should get right into it...the nausea, the dizziness, the feeling of being in a tunnel.

Now life has a way of guaranteeing such dragon-facing moments. Not a week later the hospital called us back in. Exactly the same situation. As I sat in the waiting room I could feel the attack begin—clammy hands, quickened heart beat, nausea—so I said to myself, "Okay, let's just get it over with. I'm going to throw up all over the place, then faint, and I'll just keep doing it until you get tired of the game because I know that underneath the panic everything is okay." Bam! It was gone. For good. I had put myself in the monster's mouth, climbed into the belly of the whale, and it was gone. No tranquilizers, no alcohol to numb the fear, no panic attack support groups. The fear was gone.

The third step draws from many religious traditions and is simply expressed in the saying, *"first walk a mile in his shoes."* Related to anger, what this means is that it is harder to get angry at someone when you really understand where they are coming from. I couldn't get angry at those two men who gave me the finger. They probably get verbally abused by people all the time. I was simply one face in a parade.

When I grew up, the most common form of punishment was a spanking. My mother was very good at it—she was fast and she hit hard. I never understood how she could hit us until I had my own children. Like most people whose childhoods included spankings, I swore I would never, ever hit my child. Never. And I didn't. Until the year from hell began. My son was in third grade and I was his team's soccer coach. One day he didn't show up for a soccer practice. First I was angry; then I was worried; then I was angry again. When I got home he was watching television, eating brownie mix out of a box. Through clenched teeth I asked him why he wasn't at practice. He didn't feel like going, he said. Without thinking I hit him on the shoulder. It all happened in a millisecond, and suddenly I understood. I understood how my mother, trying to raise five children on her own, could get frustrated enough to haul off and belt me a good one. It didn't make her behavior acceptable, but it put a softer light on the situation. I cried harder than my son that day—for all the ignorance and lack of empathy and patience that surrounds us. So put yourself in the other's person's place. And recognize how much the situations occur as a result of our expectations of others. Buddhism teaches us to never have expectations for other people. Just be kind to them.

Step four is to *be patient with your stumbling.* Anger goes away if it isn't treated as though it is special. In meditation we tell practitioners to simply label their angry thoughts as thinking. Don't give them any weight. Like a fire without oxygen they'll go away. Just let go. As your resistance goes, so will the negative emotions. Over time the thoughts of anger will be replaced by snippets of compassion, which slowly and steadily grow into a feeling of love...even for that person who is utterly infuriating you this very minute...even for your worst enemy. I am not saying that you will love their actions. You may never love what they do, and for good reasons. Instead, you may find that you can more effectively counteract their actions from a place of compassion than you ever could from a place of anger.

In *The Dhammapada* there is a very powerful passage: "Hate never dispels hate. Only love dispels hate." Indeed that is the lesson of the few heroes we have left—Nelson Mandela, Martin Luther King, Mother Theresa, Cesar Chavez, the Dalai Lama. They face hate with love. With patience and compassion they give us hope.

What is the result of these four steps? Does anger ever go away and stay away for good? No, it doesn't. Instead our anger becomes like lightning, powerful, illuminating, even beautiful. Best of all, it's gone in a flash. You'll see.

# Chapter Six

# On Becoming Wise

> The wise man tells you
> Where you have fallen
> And where you may fall—
> Invaluable secrets.
> Follow him, follow the way.
>
> Let him chasten and teach you
> And keep you from mischief.
> The world may hate him
> But good men love him.
>
> The wise man, following the way,
> Crosses over, beyond the reach of death....
>
> In this world the wise man
> Becomes himself a light,
> Pure, shining, and free.
> —The Dhammapada

What is wisdom? Doing the right thing in the right moment. (What a concept.) I wonder how many of us are truly wise? How many of us can say or do the right thing in the right moment? When we do, it can change the world.

I have a favorite wisdom story. I think it came out of the Judaic tradition and we Buddhists borrowed it. It's about a temple which had fallen on tough times. Over the last century, a combination of government repression, the shift to an industrial economy where everyone needed to work to pay the bills, better television programs, and a global obsession with the Internet, meant that the temple had slowly lost its members until there were only five monks living in it and they were all older than seventy. Near the temple was a little hut where a wandering monk would occasionally stay. Over the years the five old monks had learned to see the clues that the wandering monk was in the hut. Sometimes it was smoke coming from the chimney, sometimes it was just a sense that he was "in residence."

One day it occurred to them that the wandering monk might have some ideas for how they could get people to come back to the temple—in his wanderings he may have picked up some good marketing tips they could use. Maybe he could teach them how to develop a Web site. It was clear that they needed to do something since they would surely all be dead soon and they didn't want the temple to die with them.

One of the old monks volunteered to walk over to the hut one morning to ask for advice. When told of their plight, the wandering monk was very empathetic. "I know what you are going through. I see it everywhere. Almost nobody is going to the temples anymore." They wept together. Then they read several prayers and chanted for the peace and happiness of all beings. Finally it was evening and the temple monk needed to return to his four colleagues who, he knew, were anxiously waiting for his return.

The two men hugged each other. As he was leaving, the old monk looked back at the wanderer and asked, "Are you certain that there is nothing that you can tell us to save our temple?"

"No," the wandering monk replied. "I have no advice. The only thing I can tell you is that one of you is a great teacher, a teacher people have been waiting for—for more than a thousand years."

When the old monk got back to the temple his four friends surrounded him to hear the advice he had been given. "He couldn't help," they were told. "We just cried together and then read some prayers and chanted. The only thing he did say—almost in passing—was that one of us is a great teacher, someone people have been waiting for more than a thousand years."

For the next few months the five old monks thought and thought about the wandering monk's words. Did they really mean anything at all? What if he was right? What if one of them really was a great teacher? And if so, which one? Was it Paramita? He had been the leader for almost a decade. Was it Pachongwhang? He was always kind and sincere. Or perhaps Parang. She could be a real grouch when she didn't have enough sleep, but she was a hard worker and built part of the temple with her bare hands. Maybe it was Irga who was so quiet, yet always shining in her practice. No one thought it could have been Komani! She exhausted everyone with her ever-abundant energy. But it was her energy and passion that had made her a great teacher of patience and compassion. "He couldn't have meant me," each one of them thought.

As the old monks thought about his words they began to treat each other with extraordinary kindness...just in case they were dealing with the great teacher; they treated themselves with great kindness as well, because, you just never know.

Since their temple was located beside a popular hiking trail the monks still had occasional visitors—usually hikers looking for a bathroom. Over time, the hikers noticed that the temple had a special feeling about it, almost an aura of kindness and compassion. It was so palpable that they could actually feel it, although their experience of it was incredibly hard to explain back home. Still, they started to return, these bathroom users, so they could feel the feeling again. And they brought their family and friends so other people would experience the same sensation of being surrounded by kindness. And their friends brought their friends, and more family members showed up, until the hiking trail became the most popular trail in the Midwest.

Some of the hikers began to talk to the old monks and to learn from them—until one by one, people asked if they could become members of the temple. Every month it seemed that at least one more person asked about the seminary program. Within a few years the temple grew into a healthy, happy, deeply alive spiritual retreat—and the five old monks died happily ever after.

What if I told *you* that you are the great teacher? What do you think of that? So, now that the rest of us are depending on you, how can you be your wisest self? Come to think of it, who is wise really? Is it our grandparents? While mine have had their moments, my grandmother still blames my feminist notion that women are humans and have a right to a decent, safe life for all of the divorces in our extended family. How wise is that?

How about our parents? While we hopefully love and respect them, how can they really judge how we need to live our lives at this shift to a new millennium any more than we can tell our own children how to live theirs? My dad *still* wants me to marry IBM's chief legal counsel so I won't have to worry about money ever again. I don't think it has occurred to him that the counsel could be a female.

What about small children? They can teach us truckloads about spontaneity, compassion, and what to do when we're tired (sleep, whine, or cry until someone figures out it's time to put us to bed), but they appear to be pretty low on the wisdom scale. As do puppies.

Although there are teachers and ministers and therapists and mentors who may have wisdom to share, we need to do our own prework in order to begin to hear what they might be saying to us. Like the old monks, we may need to be miserable enough, or feel sufficiently cornered, or simply be old enough to *want* to listen. Happily, life beats us all up sufficiently so that something will eventually motivate us to start paying attention, to start watching for wisdom.

Won't we be surprised to find out that it's the postal worker, or the nurse in the cancer unit, or the camp counselor, or the recycling pickup person who has the most to teach us right this minute? It may not be the well-advertised, infomercialed guru-types of the world, because wisdom isn't just about saying the right words, it's about living the right words, and anyone who lives in a huge house with a big new car and lots of fancy clothes has missed a major point somewhere along the way. How do I know? Because the need to be surrounded by wealth at a time when you and I are surrounded by more poverty than has ever before existed (there are about five billion people on the planet, and most of them are poor) shows that some part of us is still protecting the ego. Ego blocks wisdom. Period. While there are some spiritual teachers that surround themselves with Mercedes as a sort of in-your-face cosmic joke, they are the rarest of exceptions.

One of the wonderful things about Shakyamuni Buddha is that once he got started on his teaching path, he didn't quit for forty-five years, which means that he left a slew of teachings behind. Many were on the subject of wisdom. As I've reread the sutras (sayings) and teachings, I would argue with anyone who would listen that he offered very clear guidelines for becoming wise and how we can build the capacity to know wisdom when we hear it. Here are three of them. The first has to do with how we each live our lives on a day-to-day basis. When our livelihood does not match our deepest values, we find life to be a constant struggle, causing us to become too exhausted to even consider the value of wisdom on a moment-to-moment basis. Within the context of the Eightfold Path, right livelihood—how we make our living—provides us with an ongoing opportunity to open our "wisdom heart."

The second guideline is to keep the faith. We need to continue to believe that a path of compassion and kindness built around a spiritual practice of prayer and/or meditation will get us where we want to go. We must be fearless *and* wise.

The third guideline, closely connected to the second one, is to learn from our own experience. Spiritual practice has the power to change our lives. Behind all that flotsam and jetsam of our thoughts is a whole huge hunk of wisdom waiting to be uncaged. Meditation and prayer are the keys.

For adults the state of our wisdom is manifested in how we spend our days, which means that our livelihood, our work, is a critical factor in our spiritual growth. Most of us unfold who we are through our work, whether it is staying at home to raise our children, working out of a home office, or working outside of our house. Because of this, our livelihood, our work, is the path we tread. It's how we participate with the universe and discover our potential. Livelihood is what opens for each of us an infinite range of experiences which have the potential to bring our hearts and our senses into full play. It is a major league wisdom-producer, a definer of who, exactly, we are. In *Zen and the Art of Making a Living,* Lawrence Boldt says it well: "What we choose to do as individuals taken together becomes what we as a society choose to do. As responsible individuals, we cannot make our career choices as if oblivious to this fact. Even if we wanted to, we could not bury our heads in the sand. The evidences of our responsibility are all around us. It is fair to say that collectively we have up to now made some rather poor choices. For currently, as a global society, we are choosing to live under the threat of nuclear terror; we are choosing to live in a world of vast inequities in the distribution of wealth and resources; we are choosing to pollute and abuse our environment, fouling air and water, forcing the extinction of thousands of species of plants and animals...." (Laurence G. Boldt, *Zen and the Art of Making a Living: A Practical Guide to Creative Career Design,* Arkana/ Penguin, New York, New York, 1993, p. vii.)

We have to choose, you and I. Will we be wise? Buddha, by the way, was not interested in anyone being poor, including you and me. St. Francis and Mother Theresa, may the Good Lord forgive me, were not his models of how to make one's livelihood in the wisest way possible. He taught that nobody should be poor because it is precisely poverty that causes immorality and crimes such as "theft, falsehood, violence, hatred, cruelty." Instead we are urged to work, because work is one of those things that gives life meaning. Regarding income, Buddha instructed that we should try to earn enough to pay our daily expenses, save enough for emergencies and our old age, and invest back into the community or our business if we are business owners.

For livelihood to nurture wisdom it needs to make deep sense to us. It needs to be in sync with our spirituality and not get in our way, because we already have lots of other things causing us to stumble. Work which promotes deceit, treachery, trickery, or usury is not going to help you move forward spiritually. And Buddha came right out and condemned dealing in arms, slavery, poisons, gambling, and intoxicants. My guess is that 2,500 years later he would urge us to be proactive, to actually create environments and businesses that promote sustainable economies, fair wages, creativity, and self-worth.

It's not easy. Many of us are well rewarded, even idolized for hurting the environment, or taking advantage of other people, or promoting violence. And we're all under pressure to own more stuff. But if we want to shift, we need to have the guts to be honest about our place in the world. Whether we are harming or we aren't. You already know where you stand. If this chapter is making you angry, then dig deeper. If you are miserable at work, dig deeper. Do you have stress-related diseases, do you suffer from depression, or are you just plain crabby all the time? The clues are obvious.

When your work matches your values, whatever your salary, you are happy. This is not to say that you are free of "bad hair days." Nobody is. Nor does it mean that your life is problem-free. Instead it's a feeling of everything being in the same playing field, that the various aspects of your life somehow match. It's a great feeling, a feeling of possibilities.

How can we shift so that our days open us to more of our own wisdom? Happily, there is an abundance of examples of people who have figured out their values and a livelihood that matches those values, and they are willing to teach the rest of us. My two favorites are Shakti Gawain and Lawrence Boldt, both prolific writers, both very wise. They tell us to watch our own proclivities for clues about what livelihood makes the most sense for us. What are we drawn to? Boldt tells us, in what is fast becoming a right livelihood bible, *Zen and the Art of Making a Living: A Practical Guide to Creative Career Design*, how to treat our development of wise livelihood as a wonderful mystery we need to figure out. Among many other things, Shakti advises us to write down our ideal livelihood scene with all the details we can muster. Then we can take time to clarify and write down our deepest values. When we know our vision and our values, we can watch for opportunities to move toward them. By the way, there is no age or time limit. In other words, it's never too late to figure this out and attempt to change it if need be. Livelihood, how we spend our days, is important up to our last breath. Robert Fritz, another teacher, tells us to simply move step by step in the direction we want to go. Start with intention and then you can move into action.

You need to believe that you can shift, that you can live a life which allows your wisdom muscles to develop and grow. Keeping the faith about anything these days can be quite a challenge. National surveys report that we don't trust much as a society. Certainly not our politicians, nor many corporations. The media isn't ranking very high and even a number of churches aren't looking so hot. Yet, keeping the faith is important. Having faith in one's practice, in the possibilities of our lives, and in each other is critical to progress. It's what keeps us going during the low periods. It's what resolves the past, surmounts our fears, and confronts whatever is holding our wisdom hostage, whether it is an obsessive love relationship or hanging onto rage at someone who abused us as children. All of the great religious leaders have taught the importance of faith, of believing in the capacity of each person to grow spiritually, living a life consistent with his or her deepest values:

*Who shall conquer this world*
*And the world of death with all its gods?*
*Who shall discover*
*The shining way of the law?*

*You shall, even as the man*
*Who seeks flowers*
*Finds the most beautiful,*
*The rarest.*

*Death overtakes the man*
*Who gathers flowers*
*When with distracted mind*
*And thirsty senses*

*He searches vainly for happiness*
*In the pleasures of the world.*
*Death fetches him away*
*As a flood carries off, a sleeping village.*

—The Dhammapada

For God's sake, for *your* sake, don't dawdle.

I remember coming downstairs one morning at the temple. It was about four-thirty in the morning. Even the birds weren't up, so it must have been in the winter. Sitting quietly in meditation I suddenly noticed the sound of rushing water, like a stream. My first reaction was to think I was hallucinating, but when the sound continued even after I slapped myself on the cheek, I turned on the light and saw that the room was flooded almost to where I was sitting. When I looked around to see where all the water had come from I found a spot on the ceiling where water was leaking—a drop at a time—from a pipe in the upstairs bathroom. One drop at a time, overnight, had created a flood. While my initial reaction, along with two other temple residents, was to spread towels all over the carpet and proceed to do our own version of Zorba the Greek folk dances to soak up the moisture, my larger reaction was to see that it was just like faith. If we just allow faith to be a part of our lives, then drop by drop we will be flooded by it. It took hours to dry the floor but I figured it was a fair price for the insight.

Faith breeds wisdom. But faith alone does not make us wise. We need prayer. We need meditation. Our first set of stumbling along this path usually focuses on silent meditation, where we are watching our breath, but over time the meditation experience itself shifts as insights start to show up. Wisdom about particular situations starts to just be there and our thinking clears.

It can take awhile to get to that point. We teach a five-week meditation course several times each year at the Ann Arbor Zen Buddhist Temple. For a full year, as a senior seminary student, I sat just behind the priest to watch how she taught the class and to learn the sequence of meditation postures. At the time, I had been meditating for several years. Suddenly, during one of the lectures, the teacher turned to me and asked how long it had taken me to be able to sit in meditation without any distractions for a full minute. I laughed and told her I still couldn't. My mind was—and often still is—this wildly careening, planning, fantasizing, worrying, analyzing, monkey mind, dragging me to the depths of despair in some moments, and to the height of ecstasy the next, with a whole lot of dull and boring stuff in between. In the moment I was asked that question I vowed to take my practice to a deeper level, to meditate more often, more seriously, and for longer periods of time.

And when I did, it changed my life. I started to see how much we really are victims of our own thoughts. And how our thinking pushes wisdom into the recesses of our hearts. I started to see that my thinking had very clear patterns. And finally, I found spaces between the thoughts where I could rest. In those spaces I finally found peace.

Of all of the masters that I have studied, I have been struck by how each one took the time to repeat to his or her disciples the importance of faith and taking time for spiritual work if we are to become wise. No one else can make us wise, they tell us. We can't pay anyone, bribe anyone, seduce anyone. Our work has only one name on it—our own.

T'aego is a fourteenth-century Korean Zen adept who became one of the country's best-known teachers. Like today, his epoch was a period when existing systems were collapsing under their own weight and people's lives were increasingly impacted by international exchanges, particularly trade. It was a time when the Mongol rule over east Asia had finally been broken and new regimes were popping up all over the place. The literature describes T'aego as a feisty social activist who earned such a widespread reputation that he was often invited to schmooze with Korea's leading politicians. Most had no idea what they were getting into. They asked T'aego to share his wisdom. Instead, he taught them about spiritual practice and the teachings of the wise. Over and over he taught that wisdom would grow out of spiritual practice and meditation, and that through persistent effort we can each discover our interconnections, our innate goodness.

In one of his lectures T'aego talked about the value of spiritual effort: "Put your attention (on your practice) and stick it in front of your eyes. Be like a hen sitting on her eggs to make sure they stay warm. Be like a cat waiting to catch a mouse. Body and mind do not move....just go on like this, more and more alert and clear, investigating closely like an infant thinking of its mother, like someone hungry longing for food, like someone thirsty thinking of water. Rest but do not stop." (*A Buddha From Korea: The Zen Teachings of T'aego*, translated with commentary by J. C. Cleary, Shambhala, Boston and Shaftesbury, 1988, p. 99)

Rest and do not stop. Our trust in ourselves gets us started. Our faith speeds us up, like oil thrown on a fire. Right livelihood helps to keep the seductions of the world at bay. Then our meditation practice can illuminate our minds, helping us to see where we have areas of budding wisdom and where there is work to be done. Many religious teachers talk about the nourishing waters of prayer and meditation. What we are nourishing is wisdom. And once you have your first taste of real wisdom, you won't want to look back. Then you're on the path for real. Wear good shoes.

# Chapter Seven

# About Teachers

*I ask Roshi to explain 'Buddha nature' to me. This is the crucial concept in our practice, the essential ground from which all being emerges, the universal truth the Buddha realized when he said, 'All beings, as they are, have the Buddha nature,' but it occurred to me during sitting this afternoon that I haven't the slightest idea what it means.*

*'Formless cannot be explained,' he snaps. He picks up the bell to dismiss me, but then he adds, 'Larry-san, your TV have Channel Two, Channel Four, Channel Five, no?'*

*'Yes, Roshi.'*

*'What Channel Zen?'*

*'I have no idea.'*

*'Channel Zero! Can any channel! Channel Two can only Channel Two, but Channel Zero can any! Understand? Listen, mathematics you have, how you say, numenator, nominator. Nominator can any number, numenator always zero. Formless, understand? Anger, delusion, insincere, even selfish, all nominator, Into zero equal zero! Your life always zero! Thought always zero! Memory always zero! You are completely free!'*

—Lawrence Shainberg, *Ambivalent Zen: A Memoir*,
Pantheon, New York, 1995, pp. 200-201.

I first saw Venerable Samu Sunim on my way into the temple to medi-tate one afternoon. Crouched over what I guessed were newspapers on the floor of the temple's bookstore was an Asian man in a tee shirt and what looked like baggy gray jeans. He glanced up at me and then went back to his work. My reaction? How nice that one of the students from the university had come over to do some volunteer work. Little did I know that he would have the most profound effect on my life of anyone I have ever known. He has seen me through earthquakes of emotional shifts and monumental struggles with my ego and my incessant need to be right. He has watched me raise a daughter, struggle with a son, and wrestle with whether I want to be a full-time monastic. He has wit-nessed my falling in and out of love, never once judging my choices or my actions. At the same time, Sunim doesn't protect. He says it like it is, working hard to translate the unspeakable into words I can understand. Always blunt, always honest. And he is just there for all of us. Always he is just there.

Venerable Samu Sunim was born in 1941, in Chinju, in the south-east of Korea. His father disappeared when he was three and his mother died when he was ten years old. At twelve years of age Sunim began his career as a wanderer, visiting various temples until he settled down to temple life at the ripe old age of fifteen. In 1958 Sunim began his official novitiate period at Namjangsa monastery, spending three years there. To this day he tells stories of the hard work, the deep friendships that emerged, and his constant hunger. In 1962, after another period of wan-dering, he went to the well-known temple of Pomo-Sa where he studied under my "Zen grandfather," Solbong Sunim. Solbong Sunim was apparently a feisty old tiger who scared the daylights out of Sunim with his gruffness, his penetrating eyes, and his repeated admonitions to con-stantly focus on the question, " What is it?" Sunim was instructed to ask the question with every breath, while sleeping or awake, in the kitchen while eating, while going to the bathroom. Nothing ever fazed Solbong, who also had a penchant for periodically disappearing into the village where he could party hard, drinking and joking, only to reappear at dawn to continue his role as a teacher.

It was through his unceasing effort and unwavering concentration that Samu Sunim was able to experience enlightenment. He is my "proof" that it is possible. There are others of course, but when it's your own teacher you can actually watch the results, "taste the dharma," as they say. The war between North and South Korea forced Sunim to leave his country, and he arrived in New York City, with only one skill: begging. So that's what he did. First up by Columbia University; then down in Greenwich Village where he was adopted by some hippies, in particular a French woman who gave him shelter. Next, his path took him to Montreal where he first started teaching in North America, and from there, Toronto. Then Ann Arbor, Chicago, and Mexico.

Although I don't know what I expected a spiritual teacher to be like, I do know that Sunim would not have been my guess. I hear the same thing from other stumblers—that the teachers they happen upon are never quite what they expected. I think we all want a combination of Santa Claus and Mother Mary, and instead we get an army drill sergeant, sometimes in drag. I knew, going into the seminary, that Sunim could trace his Zen lineage way back, because he refers to himself as the 57th generation. Which makes me a member of the 58th! Although he is small in stature, and his movements are gentle, when I think of Sunim, I think of yelling. Not just little yells, but yells that can shake a house. Once he yelled so loudly at roaches that had decided to share one of the temples that they scurried off as fast as their little legs would carry them, never to be seen again. And he yells a lot. He has yelled at everyone that I know who has been a serious student.

I remember that the second time I ever saw him was when he marched into the Ann Arbor temple on a visit from Chicago and proceeded to yell at all the mistakes he saw in the setup of the temple. "What is this?" "Why is this here?" "The matches on the altar are the wrong matches." "The bulletin board is messy." "The candles aren't being properly cared for." "Fresh flowers are needed." It seemed like he went on forever. My reaction went from anger, to defensiveness, to just wanting to argue back. Who was this guy? Didn't he know that a Zen master, a spiritual teacher, was supposed to be gentle and all wise? He or she should be beautiful and kind and always happy, not to mention thin, physically fit, and wrinkle-free since they live perfect, stress-free lives. Ah, those mental models. I was drowning in them. I wanted him to be a saint, and he wasn't, and it made me furious.

I had to laugh out loud when I first read Lawrence Shainberg's description of one of his teachers in *Ambivalent Zen*: "Kyudo Roshi wears his Yankee cap to breakfast, doesn't remove it even after we sit down. He has a large collection of hats, but he has worn this one exclusively since I bought it for him last week at Yankee Stadium. Slightly self-conscious about his shaved head, he never goes without a hat...like any Zen Master he aims to walk the streets as if invisible, attract no attention, leave no trace of himself in anyone's mind. The robes he wears in the Zendo are seldom worn outside it. He favors flannel shirts and khaki pants, Saucony running shoes, a Yankee jacket in the fall, and, when the weather turns cold, a parka and a black woolen watch cap purchased through the L. L. Bean catalog...despite the fact that he studied English in high school, (he) speaks as if he did not encounter the language until a few months ago. An expectant woman in our Zendo is "four months president." "Vagina"—a word that frequently occurs in his lectures—is "pajama." He says "minimum" for "maximum" and vice versa. One of his favorite foods is "penis butter." (*Ambivalent Zen*, pp. 3-5).

One of Sunim's favorite foods is ice cream. He tells great jokes. Some days he looks like an Asian techno-punk, a little like John Lennon in some settings. Never what I expected, but he is right there with me all the time—every minute. I get quizzed on Buddhist teachings and he gets up with me at four-forty-five to show me how to do the morning wake-up chant correctly, and after awhile, he calmly says that I would be a failure in an Asian temple. When I feel like I'll never manage the next step along the path, he reminds me that there is time, by his estimate ten thousand years, so it's probably not useful to get so frustrated. When I think I am a lousy student, he shrugs and gives me some manual work to do.

He makes me mad too. Sometimes I get so mad that I storm out of the temple vowing never to return. One of my friends told me that she got so mad at him one time that she told him to "go fuck himself" eight times in about as many minutes. She knows because when she was done his only reaction was to say, "You said 'fuck you' to me eight times." No anger. No resentment. Just stating the facts. We still laugh about it. I've cooked some of the worst food he's ever tasted and he tells me that my dharma talks need to be more gracious, more polite. He admonishes me to calm down when I'm hyper before retreats and demands to know why I am whispering to someone during a silent period. He tells me I can give more, and that I can do more. If I have decided to be a Zen warrior, then I need to act like one. I'm the one who picked the path, after all.

For the three years that I was in the seminary, there were times when I thought I had died and gone to hell. Where were Saint Theresa and Ma Meera when I needed them? A friend gave me a teddy bear so I could climb into bed with it and lick my ego wounds. I would sit on a cushion cursing at Sunim under my breath. He pushes too hard. He doesn't understand. Occasionally I would even yell back, and tell him he was rude and selfish. Leave and come back. Leave and come back. Leave and come back. I even went to different churches. But they never had the texture, the completeness, the drive, and sometimes they didn't have the compassion or wisdom.

They seemed somehow stale.

Each time I came back it was as though nothing had happened for Sunim. We were best friends. He was my dharma buddy. There was never anger in his voice; only love without end. There was never a sense of anything to forgive; only compassion, and every once in awhile, a twinkle in an eye.

Until one day, I suddenly realized in a moment, what an extraordinary teacher I had found. Someone who would teach me what I needed to learn and rub my ego raw until I finally understood what a barrier it is to spiritual progress. Someone who would teach me what real love is all about, without judgment, and what loyalty is. Whole new worlds opened up for me in that moment. All I could do was laugh out loud at how much each situation had been exquisitely orchestrated so I could watch my own "self" at work—my need to be right, to determine the rules, to decide what is or isn't important in a given situation. What a guy!

By now I've read *The Dhammapada* a hundred times. Maybe more. With the same delight that you feel when you have been walking down the same road for years and discover something you never noticed before, I am constantly delighted to find passages that feel like I am reading them for the first time. This is the one I have just discovered about teachers:

> *"The wise man tells you where you have fallen*
> *And where you yet may fall—*
> *Let him chasten and teach you and keep you from mischief."*

And so Sunim has kept me from mischief. He has guided me down this path we are all on. It was Sunim who taught me how to breathe deeply and to watch my breath, and who kept reminding me about faith. To his credit he did not laugh out loud when I proudly announced to him that I was sure I was enlightened; he instead gently suggested that the experience I was using as proof was more like a hallucination. Definitely not enlightenment. Sunim taught me how to really, really concentrate by focusing on my "bright moon mind," a spot on the floor three feet in front of me. He knew when I was ready to start concentrating on a koan, an unanswerable question which he demanded I answer. He taught me to shout from my belly and how to simply be with someone who is suffering deeply.

It was through his guidance that I discovered other teachers like Chinul, a twelfth-century Korean teacher, with whom I promptly fell in love. Chinul wasted no words with his advice, which is as practical as it gets. Chinul told his students, over and over, to keep the faith, just keep the faith, and that it is the actions that teach you about a person, not his or her words. When the words and actions contradict each other something is most definitely wrong with the picture. In those moments when I feel overwhelmed by what I know is inappropriate desire—attraction to someone who is already happily mated, for example—Chinul is the teacher who reminds me to contemplate the impurity of the body; in other words, to picture him throwing up or drooling all over the place and to hold that picture until the worst of the desire passes. It sounds weird but it works. It's been a bad year when I have seen several dozen droolers in my mind. I have also discovered that contemplating the impurity of the body also helps me to figure out if what I am feeling is simply physical desire or if there is something more. When it's more, no image is too gross. In those instances only physical distance weakens the pull.

Chinul taught me that hatred can be balanced by compassion and that I can stop being so distracted if I just count my breaths. He reminds me that the window to miracles is made up of acts of loving kindness, mine and yours, everyone's in fact. That I can always tap into the divine through such acts, and that they will always bring me comfort. Good old Chinul. You gotta love him.

Some of the most effective teachers aren't always the formal ones, and not necessarily the obviously spiritual ones. May Sarton is another person who has been a good teacher for me. One birthday I treated myself to a May Sarton book party, ending up with a series of her journals. We can learn so much about life and living when we take time to look at the world through someone else's lens. May teaches about loneliness and aging and sorrow and a deep love of nature. She has demons she has to face. She has periods of deep depression, anguish, and anxiety, and yet she keeps plodding along, occasionally pausing in a moment of rapture brought on by a glimpse of a flower in a vase or a sunset. She struggles with the power of her own ego, wrestling it down, losing to it sometimes. Then again, sometimes rapture wins out. In one of her journals she wrote: "September 15th. Begin here. It is raining. I look out on the maple, where a few leaves have turned yellow, and listen to Punch, the parrot, talking to himself and to the rain ticking gently against the windows. I am here alone for the first time in weeks, to take up my real life again at last. That is what is strange—that friends, even passionate love are not my real life....On my desk, small pink roses; strange how often the autumn roses look sad, fade quickly, frost browned at the edges! But these are lovely, bright, singing pink. On the mantel, in the Japanese jar, two sprays of white lilies, maroon pollen on the stamens, and a branch of peony leaves turned a strange pinkish-brown. It is an elegant bouquet; Shibui the Japanese would call it. When I am alone the flowers are really seen; I can pay attention to them. They are felt as presences....I am floated on their moments." Sigh. (May Sarton, *Journal of a Solitude,* W. W. Norton, New York and London, 1973, p. 11)

The stories of teachers are our own stories. They provide us with a vision of what we can experience in our own lives, when we decide to really hunker down. They teach us about pain and persistence and joy and humor. They are the legacies that we turn to in the middle of the night when we would much rather be pleasantly drunk or having raunchy sex. They remind us that life is unbelievably short and that focus is important. They motivate us. And whether we like it or not, the best ones keep us honest and rub our egos into the ground.

Do you need a teacher? Not really. There are probably millions of people who, across time, have mastered their own path without the benefit of a teacher. And there are famous stories of enlightenment or mystic experiences that happened without the benefit of someone else's coaching.

But a teacher helps. A teacher can fast-forward your stumbling; you may still stumble but you'll burn through ego at a faster pace. Society is riddled with pretend teachers, but we are also blessed with excellent authentic ones. They keep us on the path so we don't take as many side trips. They understand our fears, and our fury. Our ego gets worked over harder and faster, but at the same time, we have the protection of their moral and spiritual support whenever we need it. And on the darkest night, should our spiritual efforts scare us silly, most have telephones.

Maybe we can go the distance on our own. I just know I never would have. My mind was too busy, my need to be right too ingrained, my ego too deep, like dandelion roots. Working with a teacher has convinced me in a way I would not have learned alone (at least in this lifetime) that we all eventually make it along the path, leaving the dark beginning for the way of light. We are all eventually freed from the dark places in our hearts. I just picked sooner rather than later.

It's time to pay closer attention to bald people in baseball caps. You just never know what that bald head is capable of.

Chapter Eight

# The Incredible Importance of Tiny Moments

> "And if again, Subhuti, a son or daughter of a good family had filled this world system of 1,000 million worlds with the seven treasures, and gave it as a gift to the Tathagatas, Arhats, Fully Enlightened Ones, and if, on the other hand, someone else had taken from this discourse on dharma but one stanza of four lines, and were to demonstrate and illuminate it in full detail to others, then the latter would on the strength of this beget a greater heap of merit, immeasurable and incalculable."
> —Diamond Sutra

There you are sitting at home watching the video "Little Buddha" or a football game, when your best friend knocks on your door. Her face is shining, her eyes bright, "I've seen this person...." She is so thrilled she can hardly talk. "His words....you have to see...." Something about your friend makes you stop, turn off the television, and to decide to see whoever this person is for yourself. However, your journey is difficult. You drive to Chicago and just miss him. Then he's in Maine, so you go to

Maine—but you just miss him. Then he's in Florida. By now you are determined. You have discovered your own personal holy grail. Move over Monty Python, mine is the spiritual trek of the ages, you say to yourself. You drive twenty-four hours straight, passing the Epcot Center without stopping, even though you have wanted to visit it all your life. You continue to Miami because you've heard he's in the Keys. You are so excited you have to stop to use restrooms practically on the hour. What will he say when you see him? Will you understand his words? You're sort of scared but the excitement is stronger. Your stomach feels like the last time you rode a roller coaster or tried one of those virtual reality game rooms.

You make it to the Keys and see thousands of people walking over bridges to one of the islands, and thousands coming back. In every passing face you see anxiety, excitement, and fear; you hear arguments about what the person will say. Those coming back walk slowly, with small smiles on their faces. You almost can't look into their eyes, they are so bright. You mentally thank your friend even though you're feeling tired and dirty from the marathon drive.

As you get closer to where he is you stop, park, and start walking across the bridge with the crowd, thinking about your own life. A quick swim in the ocean clears your head and you stop to buy an offering of fruit from a very happy vendor. A walk across a park and there he is, talking quietly to a crowd of people who are listening with as much concentration as they can muster. You sit, take a deep breath, and listen. His words: "Do not let pleasure distract you from your spiritual practice. Free yourself from attachment to these things called passion and desire, lust, grief, anger, and fear. They are hindrances. Rocks in your way. Be pure, see, speak the truth, live it, do your own work. Take small steps. Focus on the tiny moments. Do good deeds, welcoming them like friends, and you will, rejoicing, pass from this life to the next."

You are stunned—you drove all those miles for this??!! First your mind kicks in. I'm not overcome with passion, desire, or lust—I haven't had sex for months, my last beer was in June, and I've been doing yoga every day, and reading about Buddhism every night. Then just as your self-righteous mind gets ready to give you that dharma army stripe you think you deserve, your heart kicks in: I drove past someone who needed help on the highway because I was so anxious to get here; I'm still mad at my father for acting like such a jerk when we were little—the man should be in jail; every time someone asks me for a favor my first reaction is irritation; John loved me but he just wasn't exciting enough—and on and on. Your heart knows, your heart hears, your heart understands the wise man's words.

Buddha was very clear in his teachings. His words can liberate the heart, filling us each with love, compassion, sympathetic joy instead of envy, equanimity instead of agitation. He keeps telling us...do good deeds, do good deeds. Small ones count. Big ones count. Medium ones count. He doesn't tell us to crawl on our knees for thousands of miles to prove our sincerity and we aren't expected to live in a cave for seven years (unless we want to, of course). Instead, we are instructed to pay attention to what is going on around us, watching for opportunities to be generous. Our very acts of generosity can keep us focused on our goal, can keep us in alignment with the divine.

When someone starts to whine about having to do good deeds, Buddha's response is straightforward. He reminds us that we can cultivate the good. If it were not possible, he would not ask us to do it, or if this cultivation were to bring harm and suffering, he would not ask us to do it. But because this cultivation brings benefit and happiness, cultivate it. Period.

The most amazing part is that he wasn't talking about grandiose gestures, although they have their place. The world will always need as many Martin Luther Kings and Mother Theresas as we can produce. In the meantime, the smallest good deeds, even the tiniest gestures can change the world. There are so many stories. The man who went out into the main plaza of his town in Bosnia and played a cello each afternoon as a reminder that beauty is possible in the midst of a horrific war; or the women I met in West Virginia who would take their children to school every morning, and then go sit in the middle of the road leading to a dump which was seeping toxic waste into the local water supply. Their daily "sit-ins" prevented trucks from dumping more hazardous waste.

Of the Buddhist stories one hears around the temple, one of my favorites is about King Asoka, who lived about a thousand years after Buddha. In the version I hear most often, Asoka believed that the way to find happiness was to conquer neighboring kingdoms. So he became a conquering fool. After one particularly bloody battle, he was standing in the middle of a field strewn with gored, limbless, sometimes headless bodies, thinking that he wasn't any happier having won a bunch of battles than he was before he ever got started. A movement out of the corner of his eye caused him to look up. It was a monk walking quietly, mindfully, and peacefully across the field. The warrior watched the monk's movements, struck by how serene he seemed.

Asoka approached the monk and asked, "Are you happy?" The monk, obviously a mendicant, dressed in tattered robes with only a begging bowl in his hands, smiled and replied, "Very." And in that moment the history of the world changed. Asoka laid down his sword, took up a spiritual path, and spread Buddhism throughout India.

Each of our lives is changed by such small moments. My memory is filled with them. Twenty years ago I was spending my high school years in a boarding school for young women just north of Sydney, Australia. To call us isolated from the world is an understatement. We were naive and innocent, completely without street smarts. It wasn't that we didn't know how to be mischievous—we did. I recall spending half my time sitting in detention for one thing or another. But being mischievous doesn't teach you how to read road maps or figure out which way is north or master subway systems.

Graduating from the school trained in every bit of etiquette that any potential debutante would be proud to know, I decided my future was in New York City, not that I had ever been there. I applied to Barnard College, and was accepted. For all sorts of dysfunctional family reasons, when it came time to find my way from Australia to Barnard, I was on my own. I was nineteen, with no understanding of urban America, no idea how to get around a big city, no sense of direction, and not a lot of money beyond my plane ticket. Although I managed to fly into New York City all right, trying to use public transportation to get to the college landed me in a totally different part of the city, way north, after dark, on no sleep for almost three days.

As I came up out of the subway system and realized that I had no idea where I was I went into a restaurant on the corner and asked how to get to Barnard. The people in the restaurant were friendly in a distant sort of way. All they could tell me was that I needed to take at least three buses in what seemed to be the wrong direction to get to the subway stop which would get me there. As they were telling me all this, a teenage girl had come in behind me and was listening to us. She followed me back out to the bus stop and sat down next to me, saying nothing. When the bus came she stood up, looked over at me, and said, "I'll take you there." And she did—three bus rides and a trip on the subway later! I was too tired to talk and I never even got her name. When we got to Barnard she just smiled and walked away, instilling in me a deep faith in the goodness of strangers, which I carry with me to this day.

Another moment. It's described in a letter I somehow never sent. "Dear Peter,

I remember the first time I saw you. I was washing dishes in the basement of the temple in Ann Arbor—my first retreat. Bone tired I stood there wishing that the dishes would dry themselves so I could get some rest. You appeared beside me, gently took a dish out of my hand, and dried it. Then you took the next and dried that one as well. I peeked up, knowing that I was supposed to keep my eyes down. It was worth the risk of several extra lives. I wanted to see who had such gentle kindness. I wanted to know who else had ended up in a place that had been so alien to me such a short while ago. Then you did it again. We were cleaning. You held the cord of the vacuum so I wouldn't trip over it trying to clean the rug without vacuuming other people's feet. Instant attentive kindness. I knew I had come home to a life that I have been looking for forever."

If it hadn't been for Peter's kindness I would have left the retreat. I was exhausted and everything seemed like more than I could handle. His small gestures kept me there, and if I hadn't stayed I would not be here and you wouldn't be reading this book. Small moments change our worlds.

I also am struck by how many miraculous "tiny moments" in my own life, and in the life-changing stories people tell me, are related to listening. So many times my life has been transformed as a result of experiencing the gift of someone really listening to me, whether it was a lover or a child, a parent or a friend. In those moments I fell into real love and had the courage to take an honest look at the way I was living my life. I forgot my fears and was able to think really clearly. A best friend once told me that world peace would happen just as soon as we all learn to listen, really listen to each other. I believe he might just be right.

Brenda Euland, one of the most prolific writers of the twentieth century with six million published words, died in 1985. Of all the words she bequeathed us, for me her greatest gift was a single newspaper column she wrote called, "Tell Me More." It was about listening and paying attention so we don't miss the message of what someone is really trying to say to us. In it she describes how we have forgotten to listen. We don't listen to our children or to those we love, much less those we don't love. And yet the people who listen to us are the ones we want to be near, in the same way that we want to feel the warmth of the sun.

> *"This is the reason: when we are listened to it creates us, makes us unfold and expand. Ideas actually begin to grow within us and come to life. You know how if a person laughs at your jokes you become funnier and funnier, and if he does not, every tiny little joke in you weakens up and dies? Well that is the principle. It makes people happy and free when they are listened to. And if you are a listener, it is the secret of having a good time in society (because everyone around you becomes lively and interesting)..." (Utne Reader,* November/December, 1992, *"Tell Me More"* by Brenda Euland, p. 104)

Those who have simply listened have given me the gift of figuring it out for myself, whatever the "it" is. I always leave them rested and lighthearted somehow knowing that we've watered my soul. I talked to my friend Alice about my marriage for hours on the phone one year. She just listened. And then I kept talking when we met in San Francisco for a weekend. And she listened and listened some more. She *listened* me into understanding that I had wrapped extraordinary expectations around my relationship with my husband, expectations that were impossible for each of us. Although the marriage later died an appropriate death, I returned home with a more realistic set of expectations not because Alice gave them to me but because she *listened* them loose.

> *"When I have this listening power, people crowd around and their heads keep turning to me as though irresistibly pulled. It is not because people are conceited and want to show off that they are drawn to me, the listener. It is because by listening I have started up their creative fountain. I do them good."*

Euland had a friend, a man, a husband, a father, a talker, a fiery force. Over the years she watched him get lonelier and lonelier, unable to do more than have a monologue with whomever ended up in the same room with him. He was incapable of listening. Once while she was visiting him, she decided that instead of pointing out his inability to listen to anyone else (we all have our moments I know, but this guy had a compulsion to interrupt someone midway through their first sentence) she would just sit and listen to him. She said nothing. She sat and just listened and listened and listened without any resistance. It took her friend several days to finally wind down, but then he finally stopped and began to listen. First to Brenda, then to other people. He was astonished to discover a whole world he had been missing. His children had grown into original, courageous, independent adults. His wife started to open up to him, again falling in love with the man who had gradually become a stranger to her. They talked and listened to each other and made each other laugh.

We can all listen. We can be creative listeners so the people around us can be recklessly themselves. We can, in fact, love them, and in so doing, offer each other and the world such moments. "And so try listening. Listen to your wife, your husband, your father, your mother, your children, your friends, to those who love you and those who don't, to those who bore you, to your enemies. It will work a small miracle. And perhaps a great one." (Euland, p. 109)

How can you start incorporating such moments into your life? How can you listen better, pay more attention? The easy answer of course is to just start. But I know from my own ragged trial runs that it is impossible to start anything when all of our waking minutes are already committed, already planned. Then we don't have time to listen, or to lean over and pick a piece of trash off the sidewalk, or give some decent food to someone who is homeless. Who among us would stop on a highway to offer help, to ask someone if they are lost, and take time to make sure that they are headed in the direction they want? Most of us don't even notice when somebody else may be in difficulty, we are so caught up in our own hectic worlds. I believe that we all have good intentions. In spite of all the Stephen King and other horror books we read, none of us was born an evil child. We all have natural compassion. If you aren't convinced, watch a bunch of little kids in action—any group of little kids. They play together, fight, wipe each others' noses, hug each other when one gets hurt, still "kiss" a hurt to make it better. Somehow by the time we are adults we have lost the time to make it better. Worse, most of us don't even notice when somebody could use that kind of a kiss or hug or cheer. We're all too busy. We want to be safe from any raw emotions—they might rub off, after all.

This business is costing us our very lives and is keeping us off our spiritual path. I was too busy to notice that my marriage was failing and that my son had discovered vodka at thirteen. I was too busy to suggest to a young friend that her boyfriend had an edginess that I had seen in abusive relationships—leaving her to discover the truth of his abuse firsthand and alone. I didn't take the time to visit my grandmother when she was dying, and I didn't go to the hospital with a friend who needed to get an AIDS test. "Too busy," I told myself. "I have matters of consequence to attend to." Today I could kick myself around the block and then some, for my needless absence.

My guess is that I am not alone. This busyness is creating a special kind of disconnectedness between us all which is deeply damaging to spiritual progress. We all progress together, or we sink together. We are as responsible for and to each other as we are to ourselves. Busyness prevents us from being aware in situations where we might make a small (or large) gesture to help, transforming the world one kindness at a time. Busyness keeps us from listening—we need to let it go.

One way to let go of busyness is simply to start creating some space in our days. As Roshi Bernie Glassman puts it in *Instructions to the Cook*, "Usually when we want to begin a new project—whether it be a new business or a new relationship or a new life—we're in a hurry. We want to jump right in and do something—anything. But the Zen cook knows that we can't prepare a meal if the kitchen is cluttered with last night's dishes. In order to see the ingredients we already have in our lives, we need to clear a space....Our lives work the same way. Just as we start cooking a meal by cleaning a kitchen, it's helpful to start the day by cleaning our mind." (Bernard Glassman and Rick Fields, *Instructions to the Cook: A Zen Master's Lessons in Living a Life that Matters,* Bell Tower, New York, 1996, pp. 27-28.)

So we create some space. In Buddhism we create the space through meditation. Just being quiet also works. No television, no music, no radio, no talking. A solitary walk, even for ten minutes, creates space and beats a McDonald's lunch hands down (no offense to Mickey D.) when it comes to giving us real energy and a calmer sense of the moment. Letting go of the shoulds we've dragged into adulthood creates space. Letting go of memberships we don't really use, and friends who aren't really friends, creates space. Limiting our volunteer work to one organization where we can dig a deep well, instead of many organizations who drown us in meetings, creates space. Limiting the number of our children and our pets and our toys and the rooms we live in creates space. Cleaning out our closets—and our basements and attics and guest rooms—creates space.

With the space we gain, our spiritual path becomes more clear, and our awareness of the whole symphony of life deepens. We can actually feel the truth of the wisdom of listening and cherishing all things, even what infuriates us: I would be soooo bored without some good, juicy, infuriating people in my life. The best ones are really smart and really opinionated. Bliss.

Space gives us the protection we need to be more adventurous. Maybe we'll skip along this path for awhile instead of taking such tiny, tentative steps. I was surprised at how the gift of space allowed me to become more focused. Over time, the focus morphed into this weird feeling of being in love with everything—trees, people, buildings, even garbage. Because they all have something to teach us. As long as I am not seduced back into being the Queen of Busyness, that feeling of love stays with me in a way that reminds me of how I've heard nuns talk about a guardian angel. It's just there. I feel safe and happy and ready to do whatever the next curve offers.

In Zen the sutra, The Metta Sutta, is a constant companion for many people. It reminds us of the importance of small moments, of our behavior and feelings toward each other. It teaches us about loving kindness, confident that we all wish for universal happiness when we get past our ego gunk. Even at my most furious, I know for example, that when my ex-husband's wife is happy, all of our lives are easier. My daughter doesn't come home in tears because of some mean comment, and I don't have to hear a second-hand lecture about something I've done wrong. The Metta Sutta promises us that when we are able to stay humble—giving up our need to be right, to control, to be angry—a natural kindness becomes available, not just to us but to all beings. We are instructed to love everything as much as a mother cherishes her only child. Everything. Not just who and what we want to love. I chanted it every day for years.

Try it. This is a sutra which can be sampled by taking several deep breaths and then reading it aloud, quietly, and with an open heart. Here is one version:

## METTA SUTTA

*This is what should be done*
*By one who is skilled in goodness,*
*And who knows the path of peace:*
*Let them be able and upright,*
*Straightforward and gentle in speech.*
*Humble and not conceited,*
*Contented and easily satisfied.*
*Unburdened with duties and frugal in their ways.*
*Peaceful and calm, and wise and skillful,*

*Not proud and demanding in nature.*
*Let them not do the slightest thing*
*That the wise would later reprove.*
*Wishing: In gladness and in safety,*
*May all beings be at ease.*
*Whatever living beings there may be;*
*Whether they are weak or strong, omitting none,*
*The great or the mighty, medium, short, or small,*
*The seen and the unseen,*
*Those living near and far away,*
*Those born and to-be-born—*
*May all beings be at ease!*
*Let none deceive another,*
*Or despise any being in any state,*
*Let none through anger or ill-will*
*Wish harm upon another.*
*Even as a mother protects with her life*
*Her child, her only child,*
*So with a boundless heart*
*Should one cherish all living beings;*
*Radiating kindness over the entire world:*
*Spreading upwards to the skies,*
*And downwards to the depths;*
*Outwards and unbounded,*
*Freed from hatred and ill-will.*
*Whether standing or walking, seated or lying down*
*Free from drowsiness,*
*One should sustain this recollection.*

# Chapter Nine

# The Invaluable Lessons of Miserable Days

Then:

*One man denies the truth.*
*Another denies his own actions.*
*Both go into the dark*
*And in the next world suffer*
*For they offend truth....*
*If you are reckless you will fall into darkness.*
*See what is.*
*See what is not.*
*Follow the way.* —The Dhammapada

Now:

*"You can't be brave if you've only had*
*wonderful things happen to you."*
—Mary Tyler Moore

*"It's a tough time. People are starving.*
*They're going nuts. It's weird. Buckle up."*
—Whoopi Goldberg at the Wilmington
College Commencement, 1996

*"We are all fleas on life's hot griddle."*
—Unknown

Yoko Ono says Americans have given the world humor. Maybe. All I know is that we do come up with some interesting expressions. "Bad hair day" is one of my favorites. I first heard it when I was about halfway through the seminary and I had one of those days where nothing, absolutely nothing went the way I had hoped or expected. First I was late waking up, and I was the one responsible for chanting the whole temple awake. I remember opening my eyes, looking at the clock which told me it was almost five AM, mumbling, "oh shit," and running full force downstairs to open the gate before anyone tried it and found themselves locked out of morning practice. I tripped over my pants and fell halfway down the stairs, picked myself up, and then walked smack into a door which I couldn't see because I hadn't bothered to flip on any light switches in my rush. Then not a single match would light when I was preparing the candles on the altar in the meditation hall, and halfway through my chanting everyone else awake I realized that I desperately needed to urinate, so I snuck into the bathroom where I proceeded to chant at the top of my lungs hoping that the other residents would think the extra sound they were hearing was rain. I forgot half the chant, I was so distracted. Then when everyone else joined me in the meditation hall for deep bows my pants slid down to my knees because I had forgotten to retie the belt in my mad dash from the bathroom. I burned the breakfast oatmeal and put too much ginseng in my tea, which made it taste like I was sucking on a filthy sock. At my grimace, the temple priest looked over at me and quietly said, "Oh, a bad hair day," and went back to drinking her tea. I thought that was a pretty funny thing for a bald person to say. And so I was introduced to the expression which would best describe my life for the next two years.

Bad hair days, I have had my share. 1994 was so full of them that I would have been better off waiting the year out in a cave.

We all have them. Why? Because they teach us valuable lessons. They teach us about the world and how it works, and they teach us about ourselves. Without them we would be lost and, trust me on this one, deeply unhappy. Without miserable days how would we ever know if we were having a good day? Without miserable days, when would we have an opportunity to practice being calm in the face of chaos and calamity? In Zen there is a saying that I usually try to keep close to me, usually as a screen saver: "Ten thousand joys, ten thousand sorrows." That's what life is. The sorrows and the joys. Without dark there is no light.

Miserable days, bad hair days, are the effect of a myriad of causes. This is one of their core teachings. When we sit quietly and consider our worst day, it is possible to see its causes—all the choices and actions and attitudes that lead up to it. I remember being deeply in love with a man who announced, eight months into our relationship, that he was returning to his ex-wife. Talk about a horrible, no good, very bad day. It hurt too much to even cry. You know the feeling. I was the most hurt I think I have ever been and the word "trust" was wiped from my vocabulary in an instant. And I was just furious. It was a thousand of my ten thousand sorrows. Later, when I was able to calm down and just sit in meditation and quietly contemplate the chain of events which led to his leaving, I saw that his decision had been utterly predictable. The arguments we had: my inflexibility about moving; her phone calls and promises; his own insecurities; their long history together. On that day I learned to see the components of situations more clearly than ever before. I learned about fear and jealousy and hope and how and who I choose for mates. I learned things I would never have learned without that experience and they were lessons which have saved my heart a thousand times since.

Ten thousand joys, ten thousand sorrows—cause and effect. This is the truth about our lives. And the days of sorrow provide an extraordinary window on what makes us tick. I had no idea I could be so angry or so hurt. There was nothing romantic about how miserable I was. For weeks I couldn't eat or sleep. Combing my hair was too much work. Clean clothes? A thing of the past. As I write I am still stunned at the impact of his action. I am also deeply grateful that I had the opportunity to learn about the consequences of my choices at a fairly early age. (And I didn't even smirk when I heard that she later married one of his best friends.) The universe takes care of things. We don't need to.

When we really look, each bad hair day teaches us unique lessons we can add to our spiritual repertoire. Here are three of my favorite (now that they're over) bad hair day stories and some of the lessons I learned from them.

Story number one: Six years ago I was invited to spend a cross-country ski weekend with some couples from a town near Ann Arbor. It was one of those "it might be business it might be pleasure" weekends where the ground rules aren't clear. I just knew that it was probably not a good idea to bring up any religious or political topics, not to mention showcasing my Buddhist prayer beads. Now I admit that I consider myself to be a good planner and am usually in a constant state of readiness for whatever life has to offer. Still, I did not completely plan for that trip since it never occurred to me that the hunting lodge-like motel where we were staying in northern Michigan in the dead of winter would have a jacuzzi. So when we all returned to the motel after a day of skiing and the rest of the group invited me to join them for a soak, I was unprepared. Thinking quickly, I went to the motel's front desk to ask if they had a lost and found. "Honey, we have something even better. We have these paper bathing suits which are good for up to three swims. And they're only five bucks." More specifically they were blue and white herringbone one-piece "play suits," just like the ones we wore when we were five (that is if you grew up before 1964), spaghetti straps and all. They were made of plastic coated paper and the packaging did indeed promise three wearings, or my money back. I decided to try one out, knowing that it would not be a pleasant picture. When I put it on I looked like some weird blue and white herringbone Chinese lantern had been pulled over the middle part of my body to protect me from some unknown evil force. I gasped every time I saw even a partial reflection of myself as I walked down the hall toward the swimming pool area.

When I reached the jacuzzi everyone else was already there. I could tell that it had been a long time since any of them had seen a Chinese lantern in human form because their conversation stopped abruptly when they saw me. I watched them try to ignore me at first, but before long they all completely gave in to staring at my cellophane attire. To give them their due, no one laughed out loud when I stepped into the jacuzzi and the whole suit filled up as though someone had pumped it full of air.

It didn't take more than a minute for everyone's jaws to close and the conversation to start again and before I knew it, a half hour of hot gossip had passed. Feeling a little light headed from the hot bubbly pool, I decided it was time to go. I stood up to leave only to be pulled back down by a man I had just been introduced to.

"Your butt's gone."

I am sure I looked at him like he was truly crazy, so he said it again.

"Your butt's gone."

I felt behind me and sure enough, the entire back side of the suit had disintegrated. Not even little cellophane frizzies remained. Nothing. Evaporado. So I did what every management consultant who has suddenly discovered that she is the only bare butt in the place would do: I calmly asked everyone if they would mind looking away (which they swear they did) while I backed out of the room.

I learned many lessons in that experience: the value of grace in a moment of deep humiliation and how being caught up in too many mental models prevented me from doing any real planning for the trip. It would have been so easy to simply call one of the couples about planned activities—a small gesture which never occurred to me. Then there was the lesson of greed. It would not have been a big deal to spend some quiet time alone. I didn't have to visit the group and I could have foregone the jacuzzi.

Story number two. My friend Mary Jo has more bad hair day stories than anyone I know. This is always a surprise to those of us who have become her friends over the years, because she just doesn't strike you as a person who has tough days. First of all, she has money, so even if she isn't working her bills get paid. Second, she is gorgeous in a blue-eyed blond, jock sort of way. She's also smart and funny. Jo is generous and kind and in many ways is a role model for the type of leadership we could use as we march into the next millennium. But in spite of all her advantages, awful things happen to her. Not big "A" awful, but embarrassing things that make great stories. In 1995 she had more rotten days than anyone else I know.

Among her stories is one which has become a sort of a mini-legend around the Midwest. When I first met her, Mary Jo was organizing a foundation in Michigan. She was also its first major donor and the key to putting together the outstanding staff and board that now run it. She really worked hard. Mary Jo is quite the businesswoman, but she is also homespun in that her lifestyle is simple and wholesome. Cloth napkins, daisies in vases, hardy work clothes, and a four-wheel-drive vehicle.

Because her life is such a motivating story she is often asked to speak publicly, which she hates to do. One evening she was sharing a stage with six national women leaders at a mega-fundraiser dinner where each speaker had been asked to share her best wisdom with the audience. Jo was the last speaker, which meant that she sat at the far end of a long formal dinner table right up on the stage. About halfway through the dinner she noticed that her napkin had fallen to the ground. She picked it up and tucked it into her waistband as she had been taught to do as a little girl.

When her turn to speak finally came, Mary Jo stood up, turned around, and started to walk to toward the center of the stage. Except she had tucked the tablecloth into her skirt, not her napkin. By the time she realized what she had done, all of the glasses, carafes, plates, spoons, coffee cups, and flowers on the table had been dragged sideways and down onto the laps of the other speakers. Suffice it to say she never did share her wisdom.

What is the lesson here? Clearly it is this: Don't believe that because you think you are paying attention to the situation you are. We all live with the delusion that we are paying full attention to the situation we are in. In truth this is rare. As a result we have experiences that may have been prevented.

Story number three. When I first started volunteering at the temple, long before my seminary years, one of the first chores I was given was to clean the temple bathrooms. So I did. When I was done and asked for something else to do, the person running the temple looked at me and said, "Clean the bathrooms." So I went back and noticed that I had really missed a lot. There was gunk around the edges of the sink and on the floor right next to the toilet, and a little nest of pubic hairs in one corner behind the door. So I cleaned some more.

When I was done I went and asked for another job to do. You know the response: "Clean the bathrooms." By now you can guess my mood. I was quickly deciding that this mild-mannered person who was giving me instructions was really some sort of sadistic freak and I had become caught in his web. But, practicing my new friend, patience, I went back. And as I looked at the bathrooms I noticed stains on the walls I had completely missed and a glob of soap by the sink well. There were still spots on the mirror I had cleaned and tiny bits of newspaper were stuck in its edges where I had hurricaned through in my initial cleaning frenzy. On this third try I took a deep breath and decided to just slow down and to clean inch by inch. I was amazed by the dirt I found. This time, when I went back to say I was leaving, the young man walked with me to the bathrooms, looked at them, and smiled. "Wonderful," he said.

I was amazed at how good I felt after cleaning the bathroom three times! I learned that paying attention, really paying attention, feels great; delicious even. It's too bad that most of us need a couple of really bad hair day experiences to learn this truth.

So miserable days have a purpose. They teach us to appreciate the softer, kinder days. We see how our practice impacts our day-to-day living. They teach us to think ahead, to pay attention and to get over ourselves because we will never, ever be perfect. These days teach us mindfulness and force us to simply stay open to the situation, watching it unfold so we can respond in a skillful way. Since they're here to stay, we might as well integrate them into our practice, making our lives somehow juicier.

# Chapter Ten

# Dealing with Rage

*"Let go of your rage.*
*Let go of your pride.*
*When you are bound by nothing*
*You go beyond sorrow.*
*Rage is a chariot careening wildly.*
*Only he who curbs his rage can be a true charioteer*
*Others merely hold the reins.*
*With gentleness, overcome rage....*
*Speak the truth.*
*Be generous.*
*Never be angry.*
*These three things will lead you*
*Into the presence of the Gods.*

—The Dhammapada, Ancient Wisdom,
Perfect Wisdom translation

Lawrence J. Lannin burned down an apartment in College Park, Maryland, killing his host's girlfriend, because she changed TV channels without asking his permission. In Denver, Colorado, Vu Phan stabbed his wife to death because she spent too much time on the telephone, talking long distance. When his two-year-old son couldn't recite a prayer properly, Aziz Safouana killed him. When another driver flashed his high beams at Baptist deacon Donald Grahamas as he was trying to pass him, the deacon shot him to death. In Vallejo, California, an argument over a ping-pong game ended when one of the players shot the other to death. James Mays shot Hal Mason to death when he beat him in a foot race at a wedding reception. Robert Clay shot his brother to death in Rockford, Illinois because he disturbed the socks in Clay's dresser drawer.

I was sitting in a line of cars waiting to pay a toll outside of Chicago. I watched a driver cut in front of a pickup truck to get ahead in line. The truck driver got out of his cab, walked up to the car, and told the driver to wait his turn. He had his hands on the car door. The driver hit his hands with what looked like a stick. The truck driver backed away, returned to his truck, opened his door, leaned in, and picked something up that I thought at first was a book. He walked back to the car and lifted what was, in fact, a pistol, which he proceeded to aim at the other driver's head. He moved his car while the rest of us held our collective breaths watching.

A strange thing happens as we stumble past the first part of our spiritual path. Just when we start to be able to see clearly, and make more out of our everyday moments, we discover that behind our anger—which we thought we had faced just fine, thank you very much—is rage. We all have it, by the way; some of us are just better pretenders than others, so it isn't obvious. My theory is that we are all totally furious that we had to be born in the first place. And if that wasn't enough, we've been sold this incredible bill of goods about life: that it will be straightforward; that we will naturally be happy; that if we work hard we'll be justly rewarded; that we'll meet that special someone; that our kids will be perfect; that we'll always be thin and young and smart; that people are fair; and that life is easy.

Of course this rage is nothing new. Our ancestors also had their moments. In Buddha's time there was a young woman named Uttara who was married to Sumana, the son of a rich man. Uttara was not happy in her husband's home because, more than anything else, she wanted to practice meditation and follow Buddha. So she went to her father and asked for his help. He sent her back home with a large sum of money. Then with her husband's permission she found a woman named Sirima who was willing to act as a stand-in wife (yes, this means what you think it means) while Uttara focused her energies on feeding Buddha and his monks when they were in town, and on her spiritual practice. One day, after Uttara had been taking care of the monks and meditating for a couple of weeks, her husband started smiling as he watched her. He said to himself, "She is so foolish. She doesn't even know how to enjoy herself any more. Look how she is exhausting herself with all this work."

Sirima, the stand-in wife, caught him smiling at his wife and became wildly jealous. Unable to control her jealous rage, she went into the kitchen and got a cauldron of boiling oil to pour over Uttara's head. When it had no effect, she went and got a second pot. Fortunately, some of the family servants saw what she was up to and prevented her from attacking Uttara a second time. She was furious that she had to share Sumana, she told them.

Clearly we can see how rage makes us crazy. When we are enraged we do things we would never have believed possible. We can kill our own children when the rage is deep enough. We can destroy our marriages, ruin our families, and even throw ourselves off of a university bell tower in the middle of a day—one of my friends did that. Once rage has its grip on us, it is always there, like a fire ready to explode up our spines and burst through our limbs, to destroy whatever it is that is causing us so much pain, including ourselves. Anger hardened into a knot that deepens and widens, even though nothing has triggered the changes—that is rage. It is an addiction to anger.

Sometimes, we are enraged for very good reasons. The problem is that its sheer strength muddies our thinking, preventing wisdom, which is precisely what we need in situations which create rage in the first place. Constructive behavior becomes impossible and we burn bridges which we might need later.

Rage can kill you, and not just through a suicide or a battle. Medical literature is filled with reports of sudden death precipitated by intense emotional stress, and rage is just that. Heart attacks, for example, account for nearly half of all deaths in the United States every year.

Many can be traced back to a person's rage, sometimes a lifetime's worth. The constant underlying hostility which is created by rage literally eats away at a person's gut, or in some cases, heart. In fact, researchers at the Duke University Medical Center, working under the direction of Dr. Redford B. Williams, have isolated deep hostility as being closely related to heart disease. More rage, more health-related problems. In a study done in 1972, 14 percent of doctors and 20 percent of lawyers who had "high hostility" scores on a personality inventory test were dead by the time they were fifty.

Medical professionals have begun to tell us that learning how to rid ourselves of rage can, in their words, "improve the prognosis," particularly for people dealing with coronary disease. Bottled-up rage has long been suspected as a cause of other illnesses as well, since it increases the levels of stress hormones circulating in the blood, upsetting the balance of the entire body. Pent-up rage not only increases blood pressure and stress hormones, it puts the nervous system into a "fight or flight" mode. Serotonin, that stuff in the brain that tells the nervous system to relax, doesn't have a chance.

What to do? Get rid of it. How? By first admitting that we all have some rage in us. For some of us that might mean giving up a lifetime of denial. Some therapists advise us to control our thoughts so they aren't angry ones. Well, I guess you can give it a shot. Distraction is often offered as another tactic. Learning to be effectively assertive so others don't take advantage of us is offered as yet another recommendation, often including training and role playing. We can cultivate friends, volunteer, exercise, get a pet, and we can pray or meditate.

Some of these methods can help, once we've admitted to ourselves that we aren't the sweet, caring, happy-go-lucky people we thought we were. But they all depend on willpower to work, and it can be really tough to stay on target. People who have been meditating for some time know that rage is much deeper than any of us ever expect it to be; like dandelions, the roots grow faster than we can pull them. It's also like poison ivy, with underground tentacles that wrap around everything they touch, strangling the heart right out of us. While a good meditation sitting can quickly soften the edges of anger, rage is different. It takes more; it demands more. It demands our recognition, our undivided attention, and our acceptance.

In the Buddhist tradition there are three practices that can help you to let go of rage. Together they have the capacity to transform you from being rage to being peace. Practicing them takes courage, and you need to be ready to make a firm commitment to weed out every last bit of rage, even if it takes the rest of your life. Ask yourself: How much has rage defined you? How much courage has it given you? Has it kept you thin? Led to business success? Is your most intimate relationship based on it? Just how big is your dependency? (If it wasn't big, the rage would have been long gone by now.)

Without a commitment to letting go of your rage, no change can happen, because you'll never make it through all the phases of withdrawal. So make the commitment. After all, we're far enough along this path by now that the deepest part of us knows that there really is no turning back. It may irritate the heck out of us, but there it is.

The first practice is **forgiveness**. I'm not talking about turning the other cheek here, or letting someone continue getting away with behavior that is unkind or cruel. Real forgiveness means grieving for what we've lost in our lives. It might have been innocence, our physical health and security, or love. It also means acknowledging how deeply hurt and angry we are about the loss. Its about letting that anger finally come to the surface of our consciousness so we can see just how furious we are and how deep that fury goes. Accepting the loss is forgiveness.

Forgiveness doesn't mean that we need to stay with an abusive partner, whatever the abuse may be. It doesn't mean that we refrain from reporting and prosecuting sexual and/or physical abuse or corruption when we see it around us. Nor does it mean that we continue to spend time with someone who calls herself our friend and yet finds something about us to criticize every time we see her.

Buddha said, "You too shall pass away. Knowing this, how can you quarrel?" You too shall pass away. Do you really want to take this rage with you? Belief in reincarnation is a real motivator here, by the way. Knowing that our consciousness is going to resurface, we really don't want to start the next round filled with rage.

Imagine that every person in the world is enlightened but you. Everyone is your teacher and they are doing just the right things to motivate you to learn whatever it is you need to know. In my life some of my best teachers have been the ones I've had to struggle to forgive. It took me twenty (okay, thirty; well actually thirty-two) years to forgive my father for abandoning my mother. Brett Butler, the comedian, needed to wait until her late twenties before she could truly embrace the damage done by her parents, to embrace and then forgive the hurts—so she could move on with her life.

Keep in mind that forgiveness is for you, *not* them. It's for *your* sake. It will help you move along your spiritual trek with a lighter lilt in your step because it frees you from rage. In a way it frees you from the invisible ties that have connected you intimately to whomever or whatever is causing your rage. You will notice that these catalysts regularly show up in your thoughts when you sit in meditation, sometimes cleverly disguised in the form of resentment, or those wild revenge fantasies we've all had. My special favorite, which showed up in most of my early retreats, was that whenever my father would apply for a new job, each potential employer would tell him that he had all the qualifications they were looking for, but unfortunately they had a policy where they couldn't hire anyone who has abandoned his or her family. Finally, he starves to death. Pretty good one, eh? I sort of miss it now that it's gone. It used to get me through the last sitting right before lunch. Now all I can do is concentrate on my koan.

*You can forgive anything.* And you need to. Not forget—forgive. Forgiveness creates the space in your heart that can then be filled with the divine.

Joan Boryshenko, a cancer cell biologist, licensed psychologist, and former instructor in medicine at the Harvard Medical School, has created a powerful meditation to help if you get stuck in your work on forgiveness. It comes from the Tibetan Buddhist tradition where skills related to the transformation of emotions are often taught. Please read it over first to make sure that you are willing to forgive. Then you can sit quietly, breathe deeply and calmly, and know that, as you forgive, so does the universe.

TONGLEN:
THE MEDITATION OF FORGIVENESS AND COMPASSION

*Close your eyes and take a stretch and
a few letting-go breaths....
Begin to notice the flow of your breathing,
allowing your body to relax and your
mind to come to rest....*

*Imagine a Great Star of Light above
your head, and feel it washing over you
like a waterfall and running through you like a river runs
through the sand
at its bottom....Allow it to carry away
any fatigue, pain, illness, or ignorance....
See these wash through the bottom of your feet into the earth
for transformation. As you are washed clean, notice that the
light within your heart begins to shine very brightly....*

*Now imagine yourself as a child,
choosing whatever age seems most
relevant to you at this time....You, better
than anyone, know the pain in your
heart at that time. Breathe it in as a
black smoke (or dark clouds) and
breathe out the light in your heart to yourself....*

*Imagine yourself as you are right now,
as if you could see yourself in a mirror.
See whatever pain or illness you have
as a black smoke around your heart.
Inhale the smoke and exhale the light
of your Higher Self....Fill your heart with light....
Bring to mind a person that you love....
Think about the pain or illness that might be in their*

*heart....Inhale*
*that pain as a black smoke, and exhale*
*the light of your own true nature back*
*into their heart.*

*Bring to mind someone whom you are*
*ready to forgive. Imagine them in as*
*much detail as you can. Imagine their pain,*
*illness, or illusion as a black smoke around their heart....*
*Breathe in*
*the smoke, and breathe back the light*
*of your own true nature into their heart.*

*Think of someplace in the world*
*where there is suffering. If possible,*
*bring a specific example of that suffering*
*to mind—a starving child, a grieving*
*parent....Breathe in the pain of that*
*suffering as a black smoke, and let it*
*part the clouds of darkness around*
*your own heart. Breathe out the light*
*of your Higher Self.*

*End with a short prayer or a short period of*
*mindful meditation. You may also want*
*to dedicate the fruits of this meditation to alleviate*
*the suffering of all beings:*
*May all beings be happy.*
*May all be free from suffering.*
*May all know the beauty of*
*their own true nature.*
*May all beings be healed.*

(Reprinted from *The Power of the Mind to Heal*, by Joan and
Miroslav Borysenko with permission of Hay House, Inc., Carlsbad,
California, 1994.)

The second practice is to **pay deep attention to what is right in front of you**. This deep attention is what keeps our focus near to us, both in time and space. By now, even if you have just tried some casual, toe-in-the-water, beginner's meditation, your ability to pay better attention has already improved. It's time to dig down, to be in this moment. Not a bad idea since this is all there really is anyway. Just now, just this. With attention, it will be possible to catch any leftover rage quickly because you will actually be able to feel it as it starts rushing up your spine.

You'll discover that there's no point in blaming. It is recognizing and then forgiving the things that have created the rage that matters. Your meditation practice will help you do that. As your stumbling improves, so will the clarity about your own life. You'll know the depth of the rage, and you'll know the possibilities that lie beyond its transformation into something you can work with—like energy. You'll know if it's the size of a mountain or the size of a football field. Pay attention but don't blame. Keep the focus intimate. What is happening to you, to your body, to your breathing? What is the real emotion behind the rage? Is it fear? Probably it is. Stare it down. Stare it down and then you can think about what you can do to not be afraid. Maybe you can move. You can press charges. You can protest. You can run for office. You can write a play about your rage, or a book. As you think about alternatives and choose one or two the rage will also shift. It will become energy, vision, and even charisma if you let it. It could make you a star, not that you want to be one of course.

One of my good friends was brutally sexually abused as a child. He spent most of his childhood in a closet, hiding from his father, in an effort to survive. He was terrified that he would either be killed by his father if he didn't have sex with him or that he would die from the sex itself. Even today, he panics if someone touches his throat or head. Dentist appointments are literal nightmares. His rage is the deepest I have ever seen—for good reason. Most people would never know it though because he is funny and kind and gentle. My only clue, for years, was that he kept getting illnesses connected with his throat and mouth. They just wouldn't quit: colds, viruses, strep throat, tonsillitis.

One day after meditating together, when we were talking about different teas or herbs that might help, he started to tell me his story. Although I have heard my share of heart-wrenching stories, this one broke me wide open. It was unimaginable, but he had somehow lived through it. We sobbed in each other's arms for hours.

Not long after that he started to paint. His first paintings were huge, bright, and splashy. Over time they changed. They were still huge and still bright and less splashy. And he began to teach children. He worked with sexually abused children, teaching them art. And some of them were healed. And he stopped getting sick in his head and throat. Amazing.

We *can* face our rage. To grow spiritually, we have to because it's a boulder on our path and we can't go around it, we have to go through. As we understand and accept our rage it disappears, teeny bit by teeny bit. It helps to watch for opportunities to assist others who are facing theirs. Not in obvious ways—that is the work of healers—but by paying attention.

The third practice is **gentleness**. Gentleness in all things. In how we talk, move, think, interact. Some of us need to learn it for the first time as adults. As one of five siblings I was well trained to be scrappy to get what I wanted or I didn't get it. Gentleness was not a part of my upbringing. So I have had to watch other people and slowly, very slowly learn from them.

Terry Dobson is a master student of aikido who has spent lots of time in Japan. One quiet spring afternoon when he was on a train in the suburbs of Tokyo, a man stumbled into his car. The man was filthy, with dried vomit on his clothes, and dead drunk. He started swinging at everyone, screaming at a little old lady that she was a "fucking old whore" and he was going to "kick her ass." While everyone else scuttled to the other end of the car, Terry stood up to deal with the drunk man. He saw Terry move and got ready to fight. Just as he made a move, a little old man sitting near them both shouted "Hey." He waved the drunk over to sit next to him and proceeded to gently talk to him about how wonderful it was to warm up a bit of sake and sit with his seventy-six-year-old wife, sipping it and watching the sun go down. As the little old man chattered away, eyes twinkling, the drunk's face softened. He ended up telling his life story, his head on the old man's shoulder. He had no wife. No clothes. No job. No home. No money. Nowhere to sleep. The little old man simply sat with him and listened, stroking his head gently. The scene had transformed itself before Terry's eyes, all because of the old fellow's gentleness.

So let go of your rage. Let go of your anger. Forgive. Pay attention. Let your own inherent gentleness free you. With these practices you can free the whole world as well.

# Chapter Eleven

# Preparing for Death

---

*"Behold your body—*
*A painted puppet, a toy,*
*Jointed and sick and full of false imaginings,*
*A shadow that shifts and fades.*
*How frail it is!*
*Frail and persistent,*
*It sickens, festers and dies.*
*Like every living thing*
*In the end it sickens and dies.*

—The Dhammapada

---

Time is taking its toll. I look down and see cellulite around my knees. I seem shorter. My waistline is almost gone. I know this because I've had to give away all my tightish skirts; I just can't get away with not buttoning the top button any more. There are gray hairs on my head. My laugh lines are permanent and I don't jump up to do prostrations any more. Instead I've developed a special ritual to get myself to the point where I am actually doing prostrations each morning. I wake up, lie in bed saying "get up" about a dozen times, do some yoga stretches (the easiest ones, the ones you can do with your eyes still closed), and then circle the spot where I do one hundred and eight to-the-floor prostrations each day. After a pregnant pause, some part of me gets the rest of me moving and I just keep moving until my mind says "One hundred and eight—good girl." I don't even try to run marathons any more. "It's not that I can't," I tell myself. "It's just that I don't feel like it—the rush of finishing a race is gone somehow." And it's not just my body that's changing. Every police person looks like a son or daughter of a friend and every schoolteacher I meet seems too young to know enough to teach. "Shouldn't they finish high school first?" I think. I know I'm going to die. It's time to start getting ready.

Friends of mine who come from India tell me that for many Indian families there is a belief that the first third of one's life is for childhood and growing up. This is followed by the second third which is taken up by marriage, employment, and raising a family. Spiritual work is the theme of the last third because it is during the later years that we have time to focus on prayer, meditation, and to deeply consider both the purpose of our lives and that death is drawing nearer.

Would that we were as wise. We need to get ready, you and I—whatever our age—because you just never know when it will be your turn to die. I remember the day I realized this. It was like getting a huge whack on the side of my head. I was walking along the Huron River in Ann Arbor, with my buddy Joy Naylor. We were two women facing middle age. First we took time to whine about aging. I don't remember which one of us said, "You know we'll be dealing with death before you know it," since I'm the one with memory lapses, but I do know that the sentence stopped us in our tracks.

So we talked about dying, about what it would be like. We decided that we weren't afraid of being dead exactly (I was lying) but we were afraid of the process of dying. What would we go through? How could I help her? How could she help me? What if one of us became a vegetable? Or had a stroke and was paralyzed? How would the other one know when it was time to get the plugs pulled—if ever?

In the middle of our walk we actually stopped to practice eye blinks for each other so we would recognize the cue to pull the damn plug. To be sure of ourselves we've been practicing our blinks ever since, usually laughing ourselves silly in the process, or crying as we feel how scary death and dying can be. Sometimes we do both.

It occurred to me, after the walk, that I didn't have the slightest idea how to help Joy or any other of my friends through the dying process. So I proceeded to become a frenzied, hyperactive data collector, spending months learning about the dying process and what the medical profession has to say about it. I think I have now read every book on death and dying in print. I searched the Internet for weeks and interviewed experts. I talked to ministers and priests from various religious traditions and went back over my own notes from the seminary. I even called my mom.

Here's what I found out: In contrast to one fascinating club that I found which simply refuses to believe in death, most of us know we will die. So, we need to prepare. We need to *acknowledge* that we will in fact die. This act somehow frees us to right many of the wrongs in our lives, making decisions which naturally lead to more peaceful days. For example, some of us apologize to our children for all the unskillfulness inherent in our parenting. We may apologize to our parents for our lack of gratitude for their hard work and sacrifices on our behalf. And we need to use our spiritual practice to help us get ready.

We are all dying. Every day brings us closer to our last one.

And what is death? Joseph Campbell talks about how the process of dying is like an old car which just stops working. After awhile its parts start breaking down until finally it simply stops. Our bodies are like that. But unlike the car, our journey continues beyond the shedding of the body, which is comforting to know. Samu Sunim once admonished me to relax when I was struggling to learn a chant as a seminary student: "You have ten thousand years to perfect it." In that moment some deep part of me relaxed, knowing that death is simply about a body breaking down, finishing its job. We go on.

The Tibetan Buddhist text, *Bardo Thodrol*, known in the West as *The Tibetan Book of the Dead*, offers the most clear instructions for how to die that I have ever encountered. In fact, it is often read out loud to a person as she is dying, and again each day for forty-nine days after death, to provide moral support for the journey the dead person still faces. In the Zen tradition we also chant for a person for forty-nine days following his or her death. If the dead person was our child, spouse, parent, or intimate friend, we may even go live in a temple for those forty-nine days so we can continuously chant, pray, and practice on behalf of the departed.

Basically our tradition teaches that a person goes through three stages, or "Bardos," in the dying process and that these Bardos take about forty-nine days to get through. The first is called the Bardo of Dying. The second is the Bardo of the True Nature of Mind. The third is the Bardo of Rebirth.

In the first, the Bardo of dying, it is important to be calm and peaceful and to pay attention to the actual experience of death. Only if our spiritual practice is mature and our meditation practice solid can we do this; otherwise fear can quickly overwhelm us. Teacher Pema Chodron tells us, "When we die we are torn out of our world. Love and hate, all our hopes and fears and all our habits of mind, all are useless."

As many people, from Betty Eadie to Scott Peck have described, white light enfolds us in this phase. It's like a mirage on a desert, a landscape of pure light. Our job is simply to rest in this light, to feel its warmth, and know its truth. Our job of living is completed and we can now relax into the next great adventure. The task before us is simply to recognize the light as the divine or the mind of all the awakened ones: "Now there is no darkness, no separation, no direction, and no shape; only brilliant light. This boundless sparkling radiance is mind, free from shadows of birth and death, free from boundaries of any other kind....all of space has dissolved into pure light."

Since most of us, when we die, have not stumbled far enough along our spiritual path to be able to concentrate on this radiance, it typically takes us about three days to understand that we are, in fact, dead. Fortunately, books exist that describe what this phase is like. *The Eagle and the Rose* is my favorite because it manages to describe the experience without terrifying the reader. When we finally realize that we are definitely dead we move into phase two, Bardo of the True Nature of Mind. The teachings tell us to let go of our clinging to the past so we can concentrate on all of the lights, sounds, and colors that surround us at this point. If we haven't honed our spiritual practice while we were alive, this letting go can be incredibly hard. But let go we must. As we do we'll see all of our residual passion, aggression, and ignorance float away and behind them will be a penetrating blue light. You'll see.

We need to concentrate as hard as we can on that blue light, ignoring the seductive white light that might also appear. Any forms that show up at this point are simply our mind's projections. If we get caught up in these projections, thinking that they are real, we are reborn. In Buddhist terms, we enter the Bardo of Rebirth, where we wait for a womb to accept us as its embryo. (I can't help thinking that this whole Bardo trip could make an excellent Woody Allen movie. Maybe it's the sitting in the Bardo Waiting Room image.) We are reborn so we can pick up where our stumbling left off. By this time, our friends and family will be over the most difficult phase of their mourning and will be going back to live their lives without us.

By the forty-ninth day we will come to the end of our journey through the Bardos and will know the features of the life we are about to begin, if we have to be reborn. Paying attention is critical:

"Listen carefully. You are now on the path of rebirth. Choose carefully where you will be born. In all the possibilities that are present for you, choose a good human birth in a good place so that you can continue on the path of liberation."

Many people have reported dying and being reborn. In fact there is a large body of evidence available. One well-known story is of a girl in India who, at the age of four, demanded that her parents take her to a village in a province so far away that they had never even heard its name. When they got there the little girl started saying hello to everyone she met in the village, calling them by name. Then she went up to a house and knocked on the door. When she was ushered in she walked up to one of the adobe walls and dug out a cookie jar filled with money which she proceeded to give to her relatives. Innumerable stories like this exist and no, I did not read them in the *National Enquirer*. Start listening for yourself. The stories will surface once you start asking around. No need to fly to India, your own community will do.

As Professor Robert Thurman, a former Tibetan monk and currently a professor at Columbia University, describes our living connection with our own deaths and future existences, we all have a subtle energy which Western scientists have not yet been able to measure. When we die this subtle energy loses its connection with our body and our specific "personhood," in other words, how we're organized into an identity, how our senses are coordinated, our thinking patterns. Yet this subtle energy is what continues. Encoded in it are all of our attributes—how generous we are, how egotistical, how compassionate, how angry. Now the attributes aren't embedded in concrete, they keep changing the same way they did when we were alive. Sort of like milk morphing to cream or cheese.

Imagine what the world would be like if we all understood this truth of cause and effect—that every single thing we do has infinite reverberations and repercussions. That everything we do can follow us beyond this life. Sort of makes you think twice before telling someone off.

This is the lesson of death. It is a lesson of cause and effect and how critical it is for us to do our spiritual work now so that it will keep us calm and alert as we die. So we will be able to "let go" of our clingingness in the Bardos and free ourselves from fear. So we can move past a need to be reborn.

For many of us, friends go first. What can we do, knowing what we now know about the death process? Well, for sure, we don't want to start preaching at them. Anyone in the middle of dying has enough people already preaching at them and giving advice and telling them what to do. What they are most often doing is introducing their own fears into the person's dying. This usually inspires clinging, usually mourning, and generally going nuts.

Our job is to be the calm one, the peaceful one, the kind one. Thanks to your spiritual practice, which is strengthening by the day, you are the one who can quietly sit, your loving kindness a gift. And you can chant. Soft chanting can have a tremendous impact on a dying person's pain and fear. The Ann Arbor Temple's priest, Sukha, tells of how her mother, a feisty, energetic, iconoclastic woman, had a difficult dying. She had cancer. Sukha still tells stories of her shock at how powerful the pain was, and how agitated her mother was, how she yelled and cried and cursed, and how scared she was. Sukha was at a real loss about what to do. So she chanted softly. She chanted and chanted and chanted, sometimes for hours at a time, and her mother slept peacefully when she did. In fact, she slept so peacefully that the rest of Sukha's family members and even the hospital's staff asked her to teach them how to chant so they could help both her mother and other patients dealing with deep pain and fear. When Sukha wasn't chanting she was meditating quietly. That brought a sense of peace to the room as well.

I find that most people who are actively dying are hungry for a sense of peacefulness and calm. Often they want us just to listen to them, to listen to their fears and lost hopes and even the fun and funny experiences of their lives. Some want hugs. A few ask for jokes—each usually dying as they have lived: The sad die sadly, the joyful ones die filled with joy, the angry ones often die angry, facing one heck of a Bardo ride.

It's tough to be there for someone else without some spiritual work behind you. I found that I was utterly terrified by death when faced with it before I had begun my spiritual practice. When a best friend told me she was dying, there wasn't anything I could do for her until I faced my own dragons. (To be honest, I still have my moments. I just sit with them now knowing that eventually they'll get bored and go away.) I watched an extraordinary parade of emotions move through my consciousness on hearing her news. You'll have them too. At first I was furious that she was dying. How dare she? We have this pact of always being there for each other and she was reneging on her end of the deal. I know it wasn't rational, but so what? That was how I felt. It took a week of long, long walks and buckets of tears to get past that fury. Interspersed with the anger were these flashes of wishes: "Maybe they are wrong, maybe she isn't really dying," although watching her physical deterioration took care of that. Then I was just sad, bone sad. The slightest thing made me sob: Driving past a cemetery, watching two people kiss, hearing about an Olympics I knew she wouldn't live to see. Finally, somewhere at the bottom of my belly, energy started to surface which had equal parts of courage and love. I knew I had what it took to see both of us through her dying. And I did.

It wasn't easy and we had some of the worst fights of our friendship. One happened because I knew I needed to set some boundaries for myself: I needed to get enough sleep and I needed daily "me" time, like

I needed to go to the movies every once in awhile. One time when I was gone she almost died without me and when I got back she swore at me with every truck driver word she had ever learned. And I cursed her back. In fact, we yelled so long and hard that we were both hoarse when it was over and I still don't know if we were laughing or crying. Probably both. But I still went home when I needed to sleep and I still took time outs for myself.

The hardest part was watching her waste away. This gorgeous, vivacious woman became so tiny I could have carried her around on my back. Her face changed. She smelled bad. Mostly her sense of humor was gone. Sometimes she just cried and I watched.

I credit my own spiritual practice with getting us both through her dying. Just being there, and paying attention, focusing on my breath. Breathing in, I concentrated on feeling peaceful. Breathing out, I concentrated on smiling—thousands of times each day, following the breath. And chanting. The soft chanting which flushed the tension out of us, helping us both to let go. Sometimes I wonder where she is right now, hoping that she doesn't become my mother next lifetime. She is so bossy she would drive me nuts.

So when it's our turn, then what? Since I've become a real "death buff" over the years I have learned that there are very practical tasks that need doing as we finish our life's work. But first the emotional stages. You'll be furious at first. It will be so strong that you'll be amazed you have it in you. You'll be madder than you've ever been. Like a Shakespearean actor, so expect to curse the heavens and everything you've ever held sacred if you think it's too soon (and most of us do). You'll probably be angry at everything and everyone around you. Sometimes this stage lasts a second. Some people never get past it. For those who do, denial usually sets in for awhile. This is not really happening to me. Someone—the doctors, my spouse, my children—is wrong. But time teaches that they aren't wrong, and then acceptance of the situation will come. I am dying. There is work to be done.

And there is. Spiritual practice includes being responsible to the people and world around us. Leaving a home and paperwork in a shambles can be an act of extraordinary selfishness. Think about it. Not only do your loved ones face mourning the loss of you, they also have to clean up after you. So do the practical work and make the decisions that have to be made. Like finding out everything you can about why you are dying. If it's a disease, find out about it. Write a will. (Actually now's a good time. How about putting the book down and writing a will right now? None of us lasts forever and death takes many of us by surprise. And while you are at it, write a living will so your body won't be superficially functioning long after your spirit has decided to move on.) Get your finances straightened out (and no, twenty is not too young), and figure out who gets what when you are gone so nobody ends up fighting over your book collection. If you have the energy, a massive garage sale is a great way to clear things out, as are donations to homeless shelters and local nonprofit organizations. The point is to get rid of all the stuff you can, while you can.

And it's never really too early to plan your own funeral or memorial service. It can actually be sort of fun. Most of my friends, even the truly pious, have asked that we have a party in their name, something I am always happy to do, although I have discovered over the years that I'm just too old now to get drunk and throw up on anyone's behalf—this body is no longer willing to pay the cost. I want a poetry-writing party myself. I want all my friends to write a poem about me and then tie them to a tree in my name. That way other people can share in the forever love we have between us and I can get one last kick out of their creativity and compassion. Then I hope everyone who has ever known me will eat a memorial (real) ice cream cone on my behalf because that's the food I'll miss the most.

With the practical tasks related to dying completed it is possible to move on to the more intimate jobs, like communicating your emotional and physical needs to your caregivers. Do you want to watch all your favorite movies? Do you want quiet? Flowers? Your bed moved? Special music? A massage? Alone time for spiritual work? And who do you want with you at the point of death? Do you want a special ritual? Holding hands, your teddy bear from when you were six, a certain song, a particular prayer? Who needs emotional closure? Can you talk or write to them? Can you forgive them and ask them to forgive you? Do it now, so the spiritual part of you doesn't have any extra baggage to drag along on your Bardo adventure.

Many people discover that completing such chores frees them to relax into the dying process itself. Spiritual practice can become more concentrated and for some there is even a growing excitement about being able to shed this old broken-down body. Unless you've been a total jerk all your life, you'll feel a sort of spaciousness that comes from knowing that you gave this life your very best shot...that you had quite a roller coaster of a ride on this mental institution of the universe we affectionately call earth. We'll all be waiting to see if we can see where you pop up next, and wondering if Polish polkas will still be your favorite thing.

# Chapter Twelve

# Egotism as a Life Handicap

*How long the night to the watchman,*
*How long the road to the weary traveler,*
*How long the wandering of many lives*
*To the fool who misses the way.*

*...he wants recognition,*
*A place before other people,*
*A place over other people.*

*Let them know my work,*
*Let everyone look to me for direction.*
*Such are his desires,*
*Such is his swelling pride....*

*Look not for recognition*
*But follow the awakened*
*And set yourself free.*

*Do not make light of your failings,*
*Saying, "What are they to me?"*
*A jug fills drop by drop.*
*So the fool becomes brimful of folly.*

—The Dhammapada

There is a story of two monks who had spent months on a pilgrimage, walking through the mountains from temple to temple, deep in their practice. While their rules of behavior were few, they were meant to be kept without question or compromise since each rule had emerged out of a thousand years of wisdom. The monks were not to take any food that was not given to them. Their last meal was to be eaten before noon. They kept silence and refrained from touching any female, thus protecting their body mind from desire.

One day during their wandering they found themselves facing a rising river which was threatening to flood the road they were on. The monks knew they had to cross quickly to get to the other side of the river before it rose any higher. They could see that the water was already up to their chests at the river's deepest point. As they made themselves ready to start crossing they noticed a young woman near them who was also starting to cross. When she got several feet into the river, its force knocked her over. She stood up and tried again but was knocked down a second time. Without a word the older of the two monks picked her up and carried her across the river, gently sitting her down on the other side. She bowed to him in gratitude and ran up the path, relieved to have made it safely across the rushing waters.

The monks continued on in silence, passing two villages and a forest. Suddenly, just before they stopped for the night, the younger monk turned on the older monk and asked him, "Why did you pick up that woman?! You have broken a serious precept! How could you have done so?" The older monk looked at the younger monk. Quietly he replied, "I only carried her across the river. You have been carrying her all day."

I am not the tantrum type. Nor do I yell or scream or whine (mostly). My way of being angry is to talk through clenched teeth, with a finely honed tone of voice which communicates to whomever I am aiming at that, in my opinion, they are the vermin of the earth, worthless and hopeless at the same time. Also stupid. This style of mine didn't survive the seminary (mostly). In disagreements with my teacher my tone went unheeded, my anger ignored. As a result I learned how to have tantrums in order to up the ante. When I thought Sunim had wronged someone I would rant about role models and Western culture and its different needs from Eastern cultures—and how right I was. I would go on and on, shaking, listing all the reasons why I knew what I was talking about, until I would have worked myself into threatening to quit and then storming off only to cool down later and realize how utterly driven by ego—as opposed to wisdom—I had been. What that man went through. I couldn't stand being wrong. Even when it made me look like a grown woman reenacting her "terrible twos" I would still rant on and on. Each time, Sunim would hear me out, sometimes simply sitting while I circled, usually saying very little. I was the worst right at the end of my last year in the seminary. Looking back I think I could have given any thirteen-year-old girl screaming at her parents for being total dorks a run for her money. Even as I write this, remembering makes me cringe.

At my ordination, in a big hall filled with well-wishers and Buddhist dignitaries from around the world, there was a final ritual where, in front of everyone, I was given a piece of advice from each of three Buddhist masters. They offered their words loudly so the audience could both witness their communication and support my following their guidance. Sunim was last. As I stood in front of him, eyeball to eyeball, newly ordained, he looked at me and said, "Parang (my Buddhist name), please learn to lose."

Learn to lose. Talk about unAmerican. But of course he was right. My ego has always been what has caused me the deepest emotional pain. Needing to prove to the world, and my family in particular, that I had married the right man. Needing to compete, to be the one who wins. And I have lots of company I think. A whole society perhaps.

From a spiritual perspective, we are all ego addicts. We all want to be right, all the time. Our kids want to be famous. So do we. We want to be special, to be noticed, to be fashion kings and queens. Writ large, the damage done is unfathomable, and we are surrounded by it. Egotism is a weed run wild. Those of us with power, even when we have our physical needs provided for, continue to be driven by an insatiable ego-hunger for more of everything. We are all hungry ghosts with bellies that can never be filled. Our egos lead to war and the harshest forms of downsizing, complete with bragging rights, and corruption only imagined by our grandparents. Compassion, loving kindness, and even justice are swallowed up in our collective need to be the one who is right, to have more, be recognized more, own more. My favorite example of ego gone awry, the presidential elections notwithstanding, is when Britain and Argentina almost had an all-out war over some tiny islands with no obvious value except to the tiny population of villagers inhabiting them. Was there something I missed?

When ego drives our life decisions we are doomed to suffering. If we marry someone because she is beautiful, what happens to us when she loses her beauty, as we all do? If we choose our mate because he is driven and will be financially successful, we may end up experiencing a loneliness we never thought possible, when we are abandoned by our driven mate. The lust for power is the worst. It makes us whores and abusers. I don't even have to tell you the stories because you know them already. And when our egos are fed we become proud, which is equally destructive. Because the pride of ego gratification blinds us to what is real. We can no longer see what is going on around us, when we're as big as blowfish and as arrogant as—let's just pick a name...how about Newt?

The Buddha offered many teachings on the dangers of ego, especially when it manifests itself as pride. In the *Ambattha Sutta* he told the story of how once he was touring a region with five hundred monks, and stopped in a Brahmin village called Icchanankala. It turned out that there was a Brahmin living nearby, I'll call him Brahmin P., who had a student Ambattha, who was truly outstanding. Ambattha could recite spiritual scriptures by memory from morning to night for weeks on end. He knew about healing and philosophy and geology. He remembered history with such detail that other historians would check with him to verify dates, times, and places going back hundreds of years.

When Brahmin P. heard that the Buddha was staying nearby, he told Ambattha to go check him out, which he did, in his own uniquely ego-driven way. Unlike all other visitors, when Ambattha was welcomed into Buddha's hut he did not bow. Instead he just walked back and forth in front of Buddha, uttering some vague words of politeness, and then just stood there, staring down at Buddha.

The Buddha looked up at him and asked, "Well now, Ambattha, would you behave like this if you were talking to venerable and learned Brahmins, teachers of teachers, as you do with me, walking and standing while I am sitting, and uttering vague words of politeness?" Full of pride, Ambattha replied that while it was true that a Brahmin should walk with a walking Brahmin, or sit with a sitting Brahmin, for shaven little ascetics like Buddha his behavior was appropriate. Buddha replied gently, "But Ambattha, you came here seeking something. Whatever it was you came for you should listen attentively to hear about it. Ambattha, you have not perfected your training. Your conceit of being trained is due to nothing but inexperience."

Well, that set Ambattha right off. He was furious and called Buddha every name he could think of, cursing and insulting him. He told Buddha that his extended family, the Sakyans, were losers. Stupid, rough, and violent. Basically lowlifes.

Buddha again. "But Ambattha, what have the Sakyans done to you?"

And Ambattha went off his head a second time. He told Buddha how he once went to a Sakyan meeting hall where he found everyone in the hall laughing and playing, and when they saw him it looked like they were making fun of him. They were also very rude, not even bothering to offer him a seat. Buddha let Ambattha go on until he was ranted out. Then he told him the truth of his own birth—that Ambattha was descended from a slave girl of the Sakyans, which meant that he had no call to put down anyone or anything. Silenced, Ambattha asked Buddha what should he do? In his response Buddha focused on the dangers of ego, and our unceasing need to feed it: "Those who are enslaved by such things are far from the attainment of the unexcelled knowledge-and-conduct which is attained by abandoning all such things." He told Ambattha that people who are driven by ego face four paths of failure. One is assuming that they will always have what they now have when there are no guarantees. In an instant all may be lost. The second failure is assuming that we can always take care of ourselves. We can't. The third is to assume that someone will take care of us. Again, this is not a given. The fourth is thinking that by simply paying homage to, or supporting, a spiritual teacher we are guaranteed spiritual growth. We aren't.

We need to let go of our egos. We need to lose. To lose our pride in accomplishments which are no more than impermanent clouds. In the losing we create a space for the divine, for our Buddha nature, to fill. We exchange pride for compassion and empathy, lust for loving kindness, anger for patience, self-righteousness for a yearning to understand.

It isn't easy. If it was we wouldn't be so addicted to our selves. In fact, because this losing thing can be tough, many of the most famous Buddhist teachers spent years and years focusing their dharma talks (sermons) on how we can let go.

One was Dogen, who lived from 1200 to 1253. With an emperor as an ancestor on his father's side and a Japanese prime minister on his mother's, Dogen was an aristocrat's aristocrat. Although he was one of Japan's best students (so good that the ruling family wanted to adopt him), Dogen was struck by spiritual fever at an early age. He traveled all over Japan and then went to China, where he meditated in the famous T'ien-T'ung monastery for two years. Unquenched, he kept searching for a teacher who could guide his work. Although he met many teachers, it wasn't until he was ready to return to his parent's home in despair that he overheard a young teacher, Ju-ching, patiently explaining to some other monks that the practice of meditation meant "dropping off both body and mind." In that moment Dogen became enlightened. In keeping with the Zen tradition, he followed Ju-ching into his room at the end of the evening and lit a stick of incense as a sign that he had experienced enlightenment. Ju-ching asked him what was going on. When Dogen told him, "Both body and mind are dropped," Ju-ching was pleased. This irritated the heck out of Dogen. He didn't want Ju-ching to be so easy to convince of his enlightenment. After all it was a great accomplishment and he had worked incredibly hard. But Ju-ching simply repeated that Dogen had really dropped body and mind until Dogen finally bowed to him in homage, reassured that his experience had been true. Dogen then hit the streets, preaching the dharma, but not in a way that one might expect. Not only was he completely uninterested in building his own ego through bragging about his own enlightenment, he was also unwilling to help anyone else build up their egos, which got him into trouble with the dynasty many times over. The king wanted his help to make the dynasty mightier, bigger, and more powerful. But Dogen had no interest in helping him. Instead he persisted in teaching anyone who would listen that spiritual practice must have as its focus studying ourselves (watching our sensations, thoughts, feeling, and actions) so that we can then "forget" ourselves. So we can forget about our ego.

Dogen preached that it is our ego which blocks our spiritual path with all its grasping need to control the uncontrollable. The mind that wants, that sets goals, that compares, is the deluded mind. The spiritual mind, in contrast, is without ego; it is our original mind. It is the mind we had before our mothers were born.

Stretch with me here. One of the central Buddhist ideas is that there really is no self. Once we start to see clearly this becomes apparent. Instead, this ego-thing, "I," that we each cling to, is simply an ever-shifting mud ball of forms, feelings, perceptions, concepts, and consciousness. This mud ball is constantly changing, sort of like those globs in a lava lamp. The problem is not only do we refuse to acknowledge that there is no actual "self," we also typically fight changes in our perceptions with everything we have. We will do anything to protect our illusion of who we are, surrounding ourselves with mental models, truisms, opinions, and specific assumptions about our futures and the futures of everyone we know. As a result we live lives filled with illusions, which as often as not have no connection with our reality. There are so many. Here's one: you'll never fall in love with anyone else because you've made formal marriage vows. As if you can control your mind and emotions, not to mention your hormones. Or another favorite: you'll never try drugs, my son, because I will be furious if you do and take away the car keys. As any parent who has tried to control his or her teenager's behavior through access to car keys knows, control is an illusion. If he's going to try drugs, he's going to try them. If she's decided to have sex she will have sex.

Still we try to control because our egos are that persistent. They are like brain weeds which grow until they run our lives completely, occasionally convincing us that our lives are working. Until some catastrophe strikes and we start to see it for what it is—a controlling bully of the worst kind.

So we practice. We meditate and meditate and meditate, and slowly, over time, the miracle happens. We are able to let go, to just let go. Then in the letting go there appears a basic openness, a basic freedom. A spacious quality that is absolutely delicious. Gradually all of our hunger to win, to be rich, stay beautiful, brag, and control erodes, bit by bit. And then even more amazing stuff happens. We feel happier. It's so strange at first because we have less, and we're happier. Our kid is on drugs and we can cope. Our intimate relationship is not exactly what we expected and that's just fine. Being president of the investment bank loses its appeal. Working with hospice becomes more appealing. We start to actually wake up happy and to go to sleep happy. Our stumbling toward enlightenment starts to feel more like gliding.

Happily, earlier generations of stumblers discovered tools that can help fast-forward this letting go. The koan, developed in early Japanese Zen, is used by many Buddhist teachers in Western society. Called a hwadu in the Korean tradition, a koan is a theme you can focus your mind on. Typically it consists of a problem or question which can't be solved with our rational minds. Most of us need to spend years intently concentrating on our koan, until all at once the experience of understanding takes place and we leap into a deep knowledge of the universe and our place in it. Often the flash of understanding happens at some unpredictable sound: a car door slamming suddenly, a bird starting to chirp, a baby laughing, water dripping. You have probably heard of some of the most famous ones:

*What is the sound of one hand clapping?*

*Does a dog have Buddha nature?*

*When you are sitting on top of a hundred-foot pole what is your next step?*

*What is this?*

*What was your face before your mother was born?*

When we are given a koan by a teacher, our job is to chew on it like a dog chews on a bone. It is with us every moment, like our skin, and we become utterly determined to discover its secret, its answer.

Here is the genius of koans. They are impossible to figure out when we are attached to our egos. It just can't happen. "I" can't solve it. So the key to unlocking the solution is to concentrate first on meditating, on calming your body-mind, and then to let go of your "self" just like Dogen prescribed a thousand years ago. And when we do—whack!— the answer is right there. We touch the divine and discover that it's been here all along, and that we are the divine. It's a cosmic joke, well worth the price of admission.

Koan work is not easy. Letting go is not easy. Helen Trorkov, the editor of Tricycle magazine, tells a touching story of a Zen nun who demonstrates how hooked we are on ego. This woman had apparently given up everything. She had left a professional job at a well known and respected scientific institute. Her head was shaved. She lived on her savings in order to spend all her time in spiritual practice, in her case helping to run a Zen center. In many ways she is a modern day role model, willing to let go of all the materialism which had defined her life. Yet when it came time to share a particular computer program she was reduced to tears.

She had found her ego's boundary. While much of her "I" had disappeared, it wasn't completely gone. It still had the strength to make her miserable.

What can we do? My vote is that we fake it til we make it, which the various twelve-step programs teach. In other words, we act as though we aren't driven by our egos, until they downsize themselves right out of our lives. It's a good idea to take time to watch tiny children in action: how they play; how they learn to walk, wobbling around like tiny drunks; how their stumbling is just part of the wild and wonderful game of life; how they instantly react to a situation with no thought of how stupid or unskillful they might look. Watch a child zoom in on a butterfly or a duck or a puppy, and then watch the puppy. That's what living without ego is like.

121

As adults we need to dig deep to remember, but when you do, I think you'll be stunned at how, even with the irritation of our dirty diapers, we were basically content, happy, in love with the world when we were tiny. We weren't having heart attacks and strokes and suffering from our immune systems giving out. We knew the answer to the koan, "What is your direct experience?" because we were living it. But as we get older, the ego moves in like a low-flying fog, causing us to forget.

If it takes sitting in the middle of a sandbox in your business suit to remember the feeling, then off you go. I'll see you there. I'll be the one in the high heels trying to get the sand out of my stockings.

# Chapter Thirteen

# The World

Then:

---

*Canticle of Brother Sun, Sister Moon*
*Most high, omnipotent,*
*good Lord, Thine are all praise, glory, honor and*
*all benedictions.*
*To Thee alone, Most High, do they belong*
*And no man is worthy to name Thee.*
*Praise be to Thee, My Lord, with all*
*Thy creatures,*
*Especially Brother Sun,*
*Who is our day and lightens us*
*therewith.*
*Beautiful is he and radiant with great*
*splendor;*
*Of Thee, Most High, he bears expression.*

*Praise be to Thee, my Lord, for sister*
*Moon, and for the stars*
*In the heavens which Thou has formed*
*bright, precious, and fair.*

*Praise be to Thee, my Lord, for*
*Brother Wind,*
*And for the air and the cloud of fair*
*and all weather*
*Through which Thou givest*
*sustenance to Thy creatures.*

*Praise be, my Lord, for Sister Water.*
*Who is most useful, humble, precious,*
*and chaste.*

*Praise be, my Lord, for Brother Fire,*
*By whom Thou lightest up the night:*
*He is beautiful, merry, robust, and strong.*

*Praise be, my Lord, for our sister,*
*Mother Earth,*
*Who sustains and governs us*
*And brings forth diverse fruits with*
*many-hued flowers and grass.*

> —St. Francis of Assisi 1181-1226.
>   Reprinted from *Deep Ecology: Living as if Nature Mattered,* by Bill Devall and George Sessions, Peregrine Smith Books, Salt Lake City, 1985

Still:

---

*"The earth is filled with love for us, and patience. Whenever she sees us suffering she will protect us. With the earth as a refuge, we need not be afraid of anything, even dying. Walking mindfully on the Earth, we are nourished by the trees, the bushes, the flowers, and the sunshine. Touching the earth is a very deep practice that can restore our peace and our joy. We are children of the Earth. We rely on the Earth and the Earth relies on us. Whether the Earth is beautiful, fresh, and green, or arid and parched, depends on our way of walking. Please touch the Earth in mindfulness, with joy and concentration. The Earth will heal you, and you will heal the Earth."*

> —Reprinted from *Touching Peace: Practicing the Art of Mindful Living* (1992) by Thich Nhat Hanh with permission of Parallax Press, Berkeley, California.

---

*"The miracle is to walk the earth."* Zen Master Lin Chi

Here's what we know: As a global civilization we seem to share this central belief in material progress which, in turn, causes all sorts of production—production of houses, of shoes, of cars, of televisions. But, this production is cutting deeply into our natural resources and poisoning our environment with its waste products. You know it. I know it. And I'm not even going to rant a la the comedian Dennis Miller about how the wealth that comes out of this production is increasingly concentrated in the countries which are already exceedingly wealthy relative to the rest of the planet. Or how, in our own country, it's increasingly concentrated in the hands of five percent or so of our population. Let's just agree that the trend is there. I'll leave the real ranting to you and people like poet Gary Snyder, a much more eloquent longtime student of Zen and nature: "The 'free world' has become economically dependent on a fantastic system of stimulation of greed which cannot be fulfilled, sexual desire which cannot be satiated, and hate which has no outlet except oneself, the persons one is supposed to love, or the revolutionary aspirations of pitiful, poverty stricken marginal societies like Cuba or Vietnam." (*The Social Face of Buddhism: An Approach to Political and Social Activism*, by Ken Jones, Wisdom Publications, London, 1989, p. 52) Others already do an outstanding job of ranting about how better than seventy-five percent of all Central American forests have been destroyed since 1975, in order to produce beef for export. Beef consumption in these countries has halved, and seventy percent of Central American children are undernourished. Dr. Helen Calicott has been showing us for years that while nuclear technology is indeed a threat to the air we all breathe, our food and water are fast becoming so polluted that the potential nuclear health hazard for each of us is child's play in comparison.

The point is that we're all connected. As some of us go, all of us go, eventually. We are deeply connected to each other and to the earth, and every move we make has an impact on others, and the more we use has an impact on others. Some of us create a little dust in our wake, some of us create lots. All of the native traditions of which I am aware lived according to the truth of interconnections, and in our own time the deep ecology movement teaches us lesson after lesson about this truth. As we start to actually experience changes in our own lives as a result of our own practice, we quickly discover the importance of understanding how deeply connected we are to one another and to the earth itself.

Why does this happen? Because clarity begets clarity and honesty begets honesty. As our spiritual chugging along opens us to personal truths, it is a natural progression to start to realize the truths of our wider community. For example, given the continued nuclear proliferation and the explosive growth in the world's population, we begin to have a sense that the world as we know it really could come to an end. Our commitment to our own spiritual progress makes it impossible for us to ignore these things.

And we want to respond because our hearts have opened up too much not to react. Arne Naess, the Norwegian philosopher who coined the term "deep ecology" in a 1973 article, "The Shallow and the Deep, Long Range Ecology Movements," talked about the connection between our spiritual work and nature: "The essence of deep ecology is to keep asking more searching questions about human life, society, and Nature as in the Western philosophical tradition of Socrates....For example, we need to ask questions like, Why do we think that economic growth and high levels of consumption are so important? The conventional answer would be to point to the economic consequences of not having economic growth. But in deep ecology, we ask whether the present society fulfills basic human needs like love and security and access to nature and, in so doing, we question our society's underlying assumptions. We ask which society, which education, which form of religion, is beneficial for all life on the planet as a whole, and then we ask further what we need to do in order to make the necessary changes." (*Deep Ecology: Living as if Nature Mattered*, by Bill Devall and George Sessions, Peregrine Smith Books, Salt Lake City, 1985, pp. 65-66)

There is a basic intuition in deep ecology that we have no right to destroy other living beings without sufficient reason. Another norm is that, with maturity, human beings will experience joy when other life forms experience joy and sorrow when other life forms experience sorrow. Not only will we feel sad when our brother or a dog or a cat feels sad, but we will grieve when living beings, including landscapes, are destroyed.

Here are some basic principles of deep ecology:

1. The well-being and flourishing of human and nonhuman life on earth have value in themselves. These values are independent of the usefulness of the nonhuman world for human purposes.

2. Richness and diversity of life forms contribute to the realization of these values and are also values in themselves.

3. Humans have no right to reduce this richness and diversity except to satisfy vital needs.

4. Because present human interference with the nonhuman world is excessive, the situation is rapidly worsening. Policies which affect basic economic, technological, and ideological structures must change.

5. The ideological change is mainly that of appreciating life quality (dwelling in situations of inherent value) rather than adhering to an increasingly higher standard of living. There is a profound difference between big and great.

What we discover, as we think about these principles that resonate deeply with Buddhism, is that the world is a system, a massive wondrous system through which we are able to realize our place in a way that extends beyond any earlier understanding we may have had. We don't just care because we're supposed to care, we care because we are a part of every single thing.

So we become the tree huggers in Northern India, fighting the deforestation of the remaining woodlands. Or we become two nurses traveling among the coca-producing villages in Brazil, teaching farmers how to raise silkworms, and thereby creating an alternative to producing cocaine. Maybe we become technology executives with a focus on developing robust recycling systems for whole cities. Or we stay put and integrate the cost of cleaning up after ourselves into our pricing for our manufactured products.

These actions grow out of a deep understanding that we are each part of a system where we depend on each other whether we like it or not. If one of us gets sick, all of us get sick. If one of us loses a child to starvation or a gang shooting, we all lose that child. Our spiritual practice helps us to wake up to the delusion of separateness with its demand to defend our made-up boundaries and its belief that we can ultimately protect ourselves by building bigger and bigger walls between our own lives and the rest of the world. In the extreme this delusion can get pretty silly. As though living in a guarded, alarm-systemed, brick-walled high-rise will protect us and our children from a drive-by gang shooting, or believing that just because a river runs through our property, we will always have water. We need to wake up before it gets worse than it already is. Our practice will give us the courage and the wisdom to do so.

When I meet people who are active in ecology-related efforts I am almost always struck by their lack of ego. "It's not me writing to congressional representatives about the loss of the water table. It's the water table protesting its inability to provide the nourishment needed by the crops here. It's the water table wanting to survive so it can quench the thirst of the seventh generation." This attitude is separateness transcended. Out of this transcendence grows extraordinary courage, the courage to see, and to tell what is seen; the courage to act, accepting whatever consequences result.

As our spiritual efforts continue, the theme of interconnectedness emerges with increasing frequency in our thoughts. It becomes a part of us as we move through each day. We make different choices: We may eat different foods, simplify our lifestyle, commit to homemade Christmases, or start carpooling. Often a different form of meditation, such as walking meditation, becomes more central to our spiritual practice. And our sense of the interconnectedness of all life deepens when we realize that it is the earth that is holding us up, not just our bones, muscles, skin, and brain.

Walking meditation is just that, walking in meditation. It has no purpose, really. It is simply walking. Because there is no goal, you will find that you tend to walk more slowly than usual. It can be done anywhere, although it is easier, when you start, to choose a place that is quiet and natural. A nearby woods, or a trail after most of the hikers have already gone home. Your back yard will do when the kids are napping; the sidewalk in front of where you live, early in the morning; a quiet city park. If none of these are available to you, then a hallway, your bedroom, or even a prison cell will do just fine. The point is simply that you are walking. If the space is small, you just turn more often, that's all.

I was taught to clasp my hands in front of me, like the children in *The Sound of Music* when they sing for their father's guests. When I practice walking meditation, unless there are crowds of people around me, which makes me feel totally stupid (I'm not that far along), I find that clasping my hands is very centering. Then, walking lightly, I breathe in first, noticing my breath. With the next step, I breathe out, noticing my breath. My eyes are down so I won't get more distracted than I already am. When you practice walking meditation, you'll find that you can't help but feel your connection with the earth, especially if you let your attention focus on the steps themselves. You have no goal, no place to go. Just walk. The earth is a huge rocking chair, protecting us, keeping us from falling into the heavens. Walk slowly. Pay attention to your breathing and you'll discover that you really are the world, as clichéd as that sounds. And you'll heal your wounds, which is what so much of spiritual practice is all about in the first place.

Our bodies and minds have wanted to heal for a long time. It's just that, until now, we haven't taken the time. "We're too busy," we whine. Deadlines and obligations and a hundred tasks staring us in the face. Sometimes, when my mind is just too agitated to sit, I turn to walking meditation for peace and am never disappointed. It slows me down and, as Sylvia Boorstein, a well-known Western Buddhist teacher, says, my mind shifts to a lower gear as my greed impulse, which is always on the lookout for something to play with, gives up, realizing that this is quiet time. My mind takes a break and I am able to find "now" and with it, peace.

Thich Nhat Hanh has written beautiful passages about the experience of walking in this way: "In daily life, our steps are burdened with anxieties and fears. Life itself seems to be a continuous chain for insecure feelings, and so our steps lose their natural easiness. Our earth is truly beautiful. There is so much graceful, natural scenery along the paths and roads around the earth! Do you know how many dirt lanes there are, lined with bamboo, or winding around scented rice fields? Do you know how many forest paths there are, paved with colorful leaves, offering cool and shade? They are all available to us, yet we cannot enjoy them because our hearts are not at ease.

Walking meditation is learning to walk again with ease. When you were about a year old, you began to walk with tottering steps. Now in practicing walking meditation you are learning to walk again ...walk like a Buddha, taking steps as the Buddha did. Each step leaves the imprint of peace, joy, and innocence on the surface of the earth, and the earth becomes the Pure Land." (Thich Nhat Hanh, "Walking," *Tricycle: The Buddhist Review*, Summer, 1996, p. 26.)

So let's walk and walk and walk and walk. Walk through our tears and our joy, our love and our hate. We can walk right through our egos and our sense of separation. Each step perfect, each step abandoned once completed. And as we do, breathe in that air that gives us life and let the sheer gratitude of being alive overwhelm us. I admit: it took awhile for walking meditation to take hold for me. At first I always felt rushed, like I didn't have time to walk slowly (funny). Then I started to resent the heck out of not having enough time to do any walking medi-tation. And then, a big surprise, I discovered a big chunk of guilt in my recognition of my own participation in the damage we are doing to the earth. Since I adore guilt, wallowing in it whenever I have the chance, it lasted for almost a year, and with it was a special sort of despair that nothing could save any of us and that we're all doomed to concrete and Styrofoam and landfill mountains and breathing through oxygen masks.

But eventually I got over myself and started to do little things which ended up having an enormous impact on my life. First I started saying no to some client work, so I could have more time to recycle, to wash my car by hand, and to walk to the grocery store. I found myself getting up earlier to walk through the neighborhood, saying good morning to all the cats who were out for their morning prowl. I discovered who had dogs and decent marriages (they were the ones still in bed) and who the enthusiastic drinkers were (from the wine bottles waiting to be recycled). Most of all I remembered what it was like to relax, just relax, with no goal in mind. My volunteering shifted to more earth-centered sorts of organizations. But the biggest shocker of all was that I just started to pick up all the trash along the curbs as I walked. Perhaps this is how eccentrics are grown. All I know is that it feels right, and I feel connected. Of course it has helped to notice that someone has started picking up the trash across the street as well. Balance. Fewer things to do in a day. More silence. More walks. Less speed. Less negativity.

In the middle of the seminary my heart was broken. I learned that a person I loved very deeply just could not make the stretch to living with an almost Buddhist priest. He tried. I tried. We tried. He left. And I was desperately hurt by it. For several weeks I kept a stiff upper lip, wrote it off as karma, and made myself busy. But thoughts of him crowded out all of my feelings of peace, and it was clear that "calm" was not going to be a part of my days for awhile. Still, I tried. I sat and sat and sat. For days I sat, trying without trying, to just let go. He has a life to live, I told myself. The sacrifices he would have had to make for me were, understandably, too high a price. He's a good man. He gave it his best shot. Even so, I couldn't shake the heartbreak, the "What did I do to deserve this?" constantly ringing in my ears, and the hollow loneliness.

Finally I turned to walking meditation. A more accurate description would be sobbing meditation. I would walk a few steps, sob, walk some more, sob, more walking, more sobbing. In an effort to prevent my neighbors from having to suffer along with me too much or from calling some health care provider to put me out of my noisy, nose-blowing misery, I finally took myself into the woods for a week, to meditate there. Walking, walking, breathing, breathing. Sobbing, sobbing, sorry for myself. I walked and walked, looking down, breathing with my steps. By the end of the first day I was cried out. By the second day I noticed the spaces between my thoughts—not happy but not sad either, and the ground felt like a soft blanket under my feet. The birds seemed to be talking to me, flying in closer and closer. Raccoons and squirrels and even deer stopped running away, although they still usually stopped. Walking. Walking. More space. Not happy. Not sad. The trees felt like they were protecting me and it was almost as though they were telling me something: Just be. Just live your life. Ten thousand joys, ten thousand sorrows. Today sorrow. Tomorrow, joy. Impermanence protects you. It is all a circle, joy, sorrow, life, death, over and over and over. Keep breathing. Keep breathing.

By the third day even the rabbits ignored me, and the woods, with the mottled sunlight and warm plant and tree smells, was home. Those woods had somehow pulled me out of my massive heartache. I wanted to hug every tree, thank every flower.

I returned home healed. No regrets. No more tears. Only loving memories, and a deeper understanding of the interpenetration of everything there is. And I understood the circle of life and death. A love affair starts, grows, matures, and eventually dies—for all of us. It may die into a deep friendship or it may die with the death of a beloved, but it always dies. All of our lives are clouds, really. We morph into rain which morphs into rivers, which become clouds, over and over. The earth teaches us these lessons. How dare we abandon it?

How can you bring it all home? Just keep practicing. Wonderful changes are taking place in you which your conscious mind can't begin to fathom. Your heart has begun to crack open and your fear is beginning to fall away. You are waking up. Walking meditation, even a little each day, provides a wonderful grounding experience. Paying attention to how you use things, and what you use, also helps. One of the traditions in most Zen centers is to take our shoes off when we enter the building. This can be a royal pain in the neck when you have just laced up your hiking boots and remember that your car keys are in the center's bookstore. The temptation to sneak in, shoed, when nobody is looking, is strong. But it is defeated by the acknowledgment of how much longer the flooring will last without hiking boot wear. Sunim has used the same razor for over fifteen years. In my house a bar of soap can last for over a year, and yes, we do consider whether or not we really need to flush the toilet before we actually do. It all adds up to being a more gentle earth voyager, conserving energy and resources when we can.

Remembering how interconnected we are helps us to be skillful in our use of materials, as will remembering that what we leave behind will either be a curse or a gift to the next generation. Nurturing loving kindness in our hearts will help us to sink more deeply and honestly into our relationship with the earth. Loving kindness teaches us about connection. In the community development movement in Sri Lanka, for example, the first few minutes of every meeting are given over to silence so that the people participating in the meeting can contemplate loving kindness, thus remembering that they are all after the same thing, a healthier life for all of us. People involved in these meetings report that such a deep emphasis on loving kindness helps them to stay motivated in their work and to let go of feelings of hostility or inadequacy.

Meditating on loving kindness can cut through your hostilities, your distancing, your forgetting how surrounded you are by blessings, whatever you are facing in this moment. There are many forms of loving kindness meditation. Joanna Macy, an environmentalist and teacher, has developed a loving kindness meditation that cuts right to my heart. Maybe it will have the same impact for you. If you read her words slowly, quietly, and just think about them, they will help you to find balance and to remember what is really important on this path.

> *"Close your eyes and begin to relax, exhaling to expel tension. Now center in on the normal flow of the breath, letting go of all extraneous thoughts as you passively watch the breathing in and breathing out....*
>
> *Now call to mind someone you love very dearly...in your mind's eye see the face of that beloved one...silently speak her or his name....Feel your love for this being, like a current of energy coming through you....Now let yourself experience how much you want this person to be free from fear, how intensely you desire that this person be released from greed and ill-will, from confusion and sorrow and the causes of suffering....That desire, in all its sincerity and strength, is Metta, the great loving-kindness....*
>
> *Continuing to feel that warm energy flow coming through the heart, see in your mind's eye those with whom you share your*

*daily life, family members, close friends and colleagues, the people you live and work with....Let them appear now as in a circle around you. Behold them one by one, silently speaking their names...and direct to each in turn that same current of loving-kindness....Among these beings may be some with whom you are uncomfortable, in conflict, or in tension. With those especially, experience your desire that each be free from fear, from hatred, free from greed, and ignorance and the causes of suffering....*

*Now allow to appear, in wider concentric circles, your relations, and your acquaintances....Let the beam of loving-kindness play on them as well, pausing on the faces that appear randomly in your mind's eye. With them as well, experience how much you want their freedom from greed, fear, hatred, and confusion, how much you want all beings to be happy....*

*Beyond them, in concentric circles that are wider yet, appear now all beings with whom you share this planet-time. Though you have not met, your lives are interconnected in ways beyond knowing. To these beings as well, direct the same powerful current of loving-kindness. Experience your desire and your intention that each awaken from fear and hatred, from greed and confusion...that all beings be released from suffering....*

*As in the ancient Buddhist meditation, we direct the loving-kindness now to all the "hungry ghosts," the restless spirits that roam in suffering, still prey to fear and confusion. May they find rest...may they rest in the great loving kindness and in the deep peace it brings....*

*Now, as if out there from interstellar distances, we turn and behold our own planet, our home....We see it suspended there in the blackness of space, blue and white jewel planet turning in the light of its sun....Slowly we approach it, drawing nearer, nearer, returning to this part of it, this region, this place....And as you approach this place, let yourself see the being you know best of all...the person it has been given you to be in this lifetime....You know this person better than anyone else does, know its pain and its hopes, know its need for love, how hard it tries....Let the face of this being, your own face, appear before you....Speak the name you are called in love....And experience with that same strong energy-current of loving-kindness, how deeply you desire that this being be free from fear, released from greed and hatred, liberated from ignorance and confusion and the causes of suffering...The great loving-kindness linking you to all beings is now directed to your own self...now know the fullness of it."*

(Reprinted from *World as Lover, World as Self* (1991) by Joanna Macy with permission of Parallax Press, Berkeley, California.)

*Amen.*

# Chapter Fourteen

# Clues to Progress

---

*"Sensory afflictions and what you think you know*
*are both barriers—*
*Totally forget knowledge and understanding,*
*do not follow others—*
*Let us go on like two fools who have forever cut off*
*the least little thing—*
*Complete realization with nothing left out:*
*We enter the family of the Buddhas."*
—T'aego

*"Seen it all, done it all. Can't remember most of it."*
—Anon.

*"How much deeper would the ocean be without*
*sponges?"* —Ditto

---

Let me say it here: Things could get worse before they get better. It isn't always true, but it happens enough for me to warn you. I meditated happily for several years waiting for the day when I could actually concentrate on something, anything, for more than five minutes. As a result, I clearly remember the day when I recognized the shift. Progress. It happened while I was living in the temple. My job was to do both the day-to-day chores related to temple upkeep, as well as what I'll call special occasion tasks. Translated into people-speak, this means that I spent a big chunk of my time washing laundry, hanging clothes on the line, scrubbing bathrooms, and washing dishes. I washed a lot of dishes. For special events, such as Buddha's birthday, I would hang banners in front of the building and deliver posters to nearby merchants, or pick up donated furniture for our annual Great Green Yard Sale. On these occasions the temple priest would often give me a long list of chores which could not possibly be done by one person in a day, given the constant interruptions of visitors and phone calls, not to mention the daily chore obligations like making beds, cleaning the kitchen, etc. Worse, I would often be instructed to do something without having any idea where the tools associated with the task were kept or whether we even had the tools in the first place. So, for example, I could be instructed to hang a huge banner with no idea whether or not we had any rope, and if we did, where it was kept, not to mention facing the tough question of how to actually hang the banner, a job for two strong people—and there was just me.

It made me crazy. I would be given a chore and minutes into it I would be furious. Just furious. My anger could last for days if indeed I was unable to hang the banner or if I never found the place where I was supposed to hang a poster. Then one Sunday morning I was asked to hang a huge wreath in the reception area of the temple. There was nothing on the wreath to hang it from and there was no "hangable" spot in the foyer. No corners. No hooks. I looked everywhere I could think of for wire, finally finding some which couldn't carry the weight of the wreath. Finally, in desperation—people were arriving for the Sunday morning service—I just set the thing down on a ledge leaning against a window, deciding that was good enough. I could feel hot anger creeping right up my spine. It had happened again. Even my cheeks were hot to the touch. But I sat down next to the wreath to meditate. To my surprise and amazement, when the meditation was over twenty-five minutes later, my anger was completely gone. It was as though it had somehow evaporated. And I could even smile at my own reaction, my own need for the people around me to be perfect. Progress.

Spiritual progress, when you are stumbling toward enlightenment, can be painfully subtle. Happily, the signs become more obvious with time as the results of your hard work take hold. But in the beginning it takes paying close attention to notice any changes. Here are the ones I've noticed the most, either in my own life or in my own Zen community. First you start to slow down. This can be very funny at first. I remember noticing some flowers in my yard for the first time. They had been planted three owners back and had blossomed each year for twenty-three years but not until I started meditating did I even notice that they had been sharing my life space. You may find that you actually have time to stop at red lights, rather than rushing through just as yellow turns to red. Of course this may not make the driver behind you particularly happy, but it is a sign of progress nonetheless. Or you may start to really taste your food and notice that you don't like lentils all that much. I started to actually feel when I was getting full during a meal, which eventually led to eating less. For me, rushing has become this big cosmic joke, and when I find myself in my rush mode I now laugh out loud, realizing I could give Charlie Chaplin a run for his money on the comedy front. My clothes last longer since I don't wreck them by rushing around in them, cooking and cleaning. Instead, I remember to change for chores (a real breakthrough for me). My fingernails don't pierce stockings, my hands find the armholes in sweaters on the first try. I don't get mascara all over everything, partly because I pay better attention, partly because I take the time to wipe the extra clumps off the brush, partly because I'm not wearing it so much any more. And for the first time in my life, I've actually been able to keep a suit wearable through four fashion seasons.

Listening becomes easier because there is time to listen and because people, especially children, become more interesting. Everyone has stories to tell. Everyone is teaching us. In listening, we figure out what their lessons are. We start to figure out what they are really saying as soon as we realize that the messages "between the lines" are as critical as the actual words being said. When someone is crying we become better at finding out what the real pain is; when someone is yelling we are able to track the real message behind all the ego noises. As someone once said to me, in our growing calmness we can "locate the ouch."

I started to sleep better. Friends tell me they have the same experience. Maybe it's just that we've stopped watching the eleven o'clock news with all its violence and anger. Maybe it's just that we don't have time to read Stephen King before bed any more. Whatever the reason, sleep becomes easier and it is deeper. I wake up rested and smiling, even on "I-want-to-go-back-to-sleep-so-I-don't-have-to-deal-with-anything" days. There's also a sort of excitement waking up each morning, an excitement that never used to be there. What will I see? Will there be a new rosebud on the bush? What will the clouds be like? Will it be rainy? What old albums will I find when I clean the closet? How will people be at the office? What were the dreams my kid had? What will be my lover's mood? How will I show her how much I appreciate her? As a part of this, we start to expect that our days will go better. And this is true even if we are actively dying. Spiritual progress gives us a calm energy which allows us to see what is in front of us and to appreciate it for whatever it is. If we're dying, we're dying. There are things that need to be done. At worst, we face a day of conscious spiritual practice.

You'll find that you also feel better. Dr. Herbert Benson, a Harvard Medical School professor, has studied the impact of meditation on people's lives for over twenty-five years. His reported results are astounding. People who practice meditation, or do some form of contemplative prayer, decrease their visits to health maintenance organizations by more than a third. When couples facing infertility work meditation into their everyday lives, nearly forty percent end up conceiving within six months. It turns out that meditation can trigger the mind to work like a drug, relieving symptoms of disease, lowering blood pressure, and alleviating and even healing stress-related illnesses. Dr. Benson's studies have been so convincing that he receives five or six phone calls each week from health maintenance organizations who want to incorporate meditation into their treatment programs.

In Western society we are all dealing with chronic anxiety. All of our mothers worry, so we have learned to worry as well. My own mother is the best worrier I know—really excellent. She has raised worrying to a fine art. Just about everything can worry her if she sets her mind to it. She worried when I started driving, worried when I went away to school, worried when I married, worried when I unmarried. She worried when I had kids, now she worries about the kids. When my daughter and I moved next door to a family with a Doberman she was beside herself. It didn't matter that the dog was the sweetest, most gentle dog we had ever encountered. She was sure that someday when we weren't paying attention it was going to rip us to shreds, pulling our limbs from their sockets for fun. Territory is territory, my mother said, and the minute either of us stepped onto its lawn it would be all over— we were as good as dead. (I didn't tell her that we used to go over and give him our leftover breakfast scraps each morning; she would have moved in!) And she worries about money. Growing up, when we weren't rich, she worried about money. There was never enough. For a time, when we were rich, she worried about money. There still wasn't enough.

So I was well trained by one of the best worriers this great nation has ever produced, and I must say without false modesty that I can be quite good at it. And yes, I have stayed awake for nights on end listening for my daughter's last breath when she goes to sleep with a cold. Even though I was a moneymaker for the management consulting firm I worked for, I still worried that I would be fired without warning. I've worried about chronic disease and I wouldn't be my mother's daughter if I didn't worry about money.

Spiritual practice transforms worry. In my case, I first started noticing how much I was worrying. Then I started to simply sit with the worry, sometimes playing it out in my mind. In Zen we say that if our minds have put us into a fire, then our job is to sit in the middle of it and get good and hot. I discovered that when I stayed with the worries, following them to their natural conclusion, they were either so outrageous or so funny that they simply evaporated. And this happened again and again. Then I noticed that I was worrying less and less. Although my days, even now, aren't completely worry free—this is a very deep weed embedded in my brain—I do find myself surprised when a worry surfaces. Typically, it moves through my system pretty quickly.

You *can* catch your worries earlier with spiritual practice, before they become obsessions. And you better understand them as you notice what it is that triggers them. Is it a phone call from your father? A card in the mail to your mate from one of his ex-lovers? A memo from the company president saying that there could be more layoffs this fiscal year? I am not promising that the misfortunes of our lives all disappear—they don't. It's just that we waste less time and energy worrying about them and instead are better able to do something constructive when faced with a difficult situation. We're able to calmly sit through phone calls, mostly listen with compassion-filled hearts, and communicate our caring without getting sucked into negative emotions. For example, when our mate gets that card we see that it is simply a card and not an affair and we realize that our best defense is to be happy and grateful for our relationship. (Besides he probably just sent it to himself to see our reaction.) And the boss's memo? It's never too early to spruce up a resumé and check in with your network or skim the employment ads or check in with your friendly neighborhood headhunter. We discover that doing something actively about a situation beats worrying hands down.

So these are some early signs. While we don't all have these experiences, most of us have at least some of them. You will too. Just stick with your meditation. At the next level—not that there is really a formal next level—the changes can be stronger. The most amazing shift for me was an overwhelming sensation of feeling safe. It started to show up when I began each sitting taking the "three refuges": Buddha, his teachings (dharma), and the community of monks, nuns, lay brothers, and lay sisters (sangha). Taking refuge means that I am committing myself to following the Buddha's footsteps as best I can; that I promise to respect and learn from his teachings; that I'll do my best to support our earthly community. It's sort of a Buddhist scout creed. Taking refuge in Buddha, dharma, and sangha also means that I choose to believe that I can trust Buddha, his teachings, and the community to watch out for me and care for me and keep my stumbling strong. For years I have taken refuge in these three jewels. Eventually I noticed this feeling of safety that would sweep over me as I contemplated the words, sort of like a warm fuzzy blanket on a shivering child. So I feel safe. My whole life is unfolding within the great arms of the Buddha. With that feeling of safety there has been a corresponding drop in fear. In fact, it's gone. Well, mostly anyway. I still freak at the idea of getting a tooth capped, a reminder that habits die hard.

With safety comes an increase in self-esteem. We can look around and see what is working in our lives and what isn't, and know that we deserve better. You know, we have a right and an obligation to be happy. This is not necessarily a right to wealth, or to constant health. It's more of a deep relaxation into whatever cards we are being dealt, vowing to pay attention and traverse each moment with as much compassion, equanimity, and sympathetic joy as we can muster.

With self-esteem, we can do our best psychological healing—sometimes alone, sometimes with help. We are able to flesh out false fears and the obsessions they create. We can see situations clearly and how a slight tweak here or there will make them more palatable. And if they are more palatable for us, they are usually more palatable to the people around us.

As spiritual practice becomes a part of their every day life, I often see people make major life shifts. They change careers or end their careers and switch to volunteer work. They stay home to raise their children, or care for an aging parent instead of sending him or her to a home or institution. I've seen people shed, and I mean shed, weight they have been carrying around for years. It's as though they no longer need all those protective layers. Some people move or go off somewhere to spend some time in intensive practice. A deep simplifying takes place. The second house gets sold or the move is to an apartment; the basement finally gets cleaned out; traveling decreases; the parties slack off; driving in the car in silence becomes the norm.

For me, this "stage" of deepening practice had profound effects on how I lived my life. The need to be mated, that obsessed drive to share every day and night with that special person disappeared. I don't know where it went, or when it went; I just know it's gone. In its place is a feeling of being happy to be with everyone I meet—beggar, cop, television producer, minister—and this happiness wishes them well, whether they are spending their time with me or somebody else. This shift alone has made all the years of practice worthwhile. Being able to read *Cosmo* without wanting to be thinner and have sex, or being able to spend four days alone at the San Diego Hyatt at the height of the honeymoon season without any loneliness, are both testimonials to the transformational power of truly spiritual work. Oh, I still have my moments. There is a builder in Ann Arbor who still leaves me in a sweat. Now I just get a huge kick out of it, enjoying the moment and letting it go.

I see people take risks that they never would have taken had they not been on a spiritual trek: A psychologist who decided to go back to school to become a gardener; a government administrator who, at the ripe old age of fifty-one, joined the Peace Corps; a young man who openly wrestled with his practice, finally embracing his own homosexuality after years of trying to squelch it so as not to humiliate his parents; a woman who took a year of absence from her life to clean up at Betty Ford; a man who did the same, only he headed for the Carolinas.

All are signs of progress. To be sure, not all signs are immediately positive or pleasant. When you start to see clearly and fear drops away, you can find yourself confronting people and/or issues that you have managed to avoid for years. I've heard hundreds of stories of confrontations with parents over the wounds their drug, alcohol, or sexual abuse caused. The horror of these addictions and their impact on us can and does surface in meditation practice. If it's part of your life, I assure you that it will bubble up to your consciousness until you deal with it. The gift of spiritual progress is that somehow a stream of fearlessness also finds its way to your conscious, giving you the courage to shake these frigging dragons loose. One friend finally confronted her brother for sexually abusing her from the time she was twelve. He didn't remember any of it until she talked him through the details. Now they continue to sew their open wounds closed.

Want more signs? You might feel flashes of joy. If you haven't had a lot of experience with joy, this can be pretty amazing and wonderful. I vividly remember my first flash, it was such a shock. I was walking across a footbridge on the University of Michigan campus. It was one of those cold, gray November days when people don't walk, they scurry. I'm always cold because I refuse to admit it's winter until the temperature falls below zero, which means that I am typically walking around with a sweatshirt and thick sweater until I'm threatened with frostbite. I remember walking onto the bridge, softly chanting to myself. I was smiling, I think. Suddenly I could feel this warmth wash over my body and suddenly I was really, really happy. Everything made me happy. The crisp cold air, the youth and energy of the students, the birds flying south. It was sort of orgasmic without the sex, if you can imagine that. I suddenly realized that what I was feeling was joy. The sheer joy of being alive, and of having this incredible opportunity to learn the lessons life was putting in front of me. The feeling stayed with me all day and there have many joy-filled days since. Although none of them have happened at the dentist's office, I'm optimistic.

Calmness is another sign. Calmness is the ether I breathe. It's becoming my living state. I can be excited and still feel the calmness behind it. I can be scared and still feel the calmness behind it. Everything is OK. My job is to stay with what is right in front of me and deal with it, using all the wisdom I can muster.

Beyond the calmness there is a sense that signs don't matter in the end. In their own way, they are still connected to ego. Like fashion and youth and Hurricane Hannah, they come and go. There is no sense depending on them or in looking too hard to see if they are there because it doesn't matter. There is just practice, loving kindness, sympathetic joy, and calm. Some people like you. Some people don't. It doesn't matter. If your career ladder falls over, another opportunity will surface. Your children's lives will take many major U-turns, but you can just be there with them, loving them, just being the best parent you can be—letting go of your need to control them. There is just practice. Deeper and deeper practice. All of the emotions come and go. Watching them, sometimes we laugh, sometimes we cry. The signs stop mattering because our own experience has taught us the value of this wonderfully clumsy fool's walk, this drunken stumbling, sometimes blind, sometimes deaf.

And after that? I don't know. I'm not there.

# Chapter Fifteen

# The Art of Cultivating Sympathetic Joy

Live in joy,
In Love, even among those who hate.

Live in joy,
In health,
Even among the afflicted.

Live in joy,
In peace,
Even among the troubled.

Live in joy,
Without possessions, like the shining ones.

Let go of winning and losing
And find joy.

Health, contentment, and trust
Are your greatest possessions,
And freedom your greatest joy.

Look within.
Be still.
Free from fear and attachment,

*Know the sweet joy of the way.*
*How joyful to look upon the awakened*
*And to keep company with the wise...*
*Follow, then the shining ones.*
*Follow them*
*As the moon follows the path of the stars.*

—The Dhammapada

---

First for yourself, then others. First joy, then sympathetic joy. Many of the people who are attracted to a spiritual practice that is personally defined—in other words, it's not someone else's job to provide the keys to heaven, however they define it—are social activists. In my own community there are people working on welfare reform, animal rights, or shifting their own corporation toward more compassionate norms. They are friends of the court, consumer advocates, nurses and doctors in the hospice movement. To a person, they are compassionate and committed to doing what they can so you and I have roofs over our heads, food on our table, clothes on our bodies, and a toxin-free environment.

Many of them are also very angry. And while anger is often the rational response to what they are each working to address, it also uses up energy they need for both their spiritual practice and their work. As an example of what I mean, Hugh Delehanty, the editor of the *Utne Reader*, tells the story of his friend James Thornton, who was a litigator for the Natural Resources Defense Council for ten years, winning more than one hundred cases in that period. Somewhere along the way he realized that the tools that the environmental movement has at its disposal are no match for the global ecological crisis we all face. According to Delehanty, James spent fourteen months searching for a way to integrate his two passions, earth and spirit, in the face of this realization. He even went to the Dalai Lama for counsel. The Dalai Lama advised him "to become confident and positive in yourself and then you can help others become confident and positive. A long-term solution can't be based on anger." First for yourself, then others. James realized that anger really was what motivated him and many of his colleagues, and it was corroding the movement. So he shifted, forming an organization called Positive Futures to help ecologists to develop a more enlightened perspective regarding what they are trying to accomplish.

Buddha was very clear about the power of the positive to have an impact on everything around us. "No matter what, live in joy. When there is hate, live in joy. When there is trouble, live in joy." Let go of winning and losing and do what is right in front of you with as much skillfulness and compassion as you can muster. Live in joy. Life is what it is.

This is not easy. (Now there's an understatement.) Most of us think of joy as that perfect relationship, meal, orgasm, business deal, court case ruling, political win. It is none of those things. Joy is intense happiness. Your whole body can feel it, not just your mind. It is satisfaction. It is acceptance. To be joyful is to be happy—and then some. It is virtually impossible to be angry and feel joy at the same time; to worry and be joyful; to be fearful and joyful.

Living our lives with joy is a moral obligation, not in the sense of denial but as deep acceptance of what our life is about, whatever our experience of it. We are content, but getting there is tough. That's why we stumble on this spiritual path we've chosen instead of stepping onto a Concorde, which will fly us there in four hours.

The place to start is to *want* it, to want to live a life of joy. Buddhist scriptures have a way of repeating themes over and over until they sink in. One of the core themes is this: enlightenment comes with joy. First for you. Then for others. So we start with acceptance of ourselves. None of us, for example, has a perfect body. Even when I was a dancer, my thighs always filled a chair when I sat down. Childbirth left me with a pot belly and serious scars. I call them my motherhood tattoos. We all, each one of us, make mistakes that can last for the rest of our lives and have moments when we meant to tell the truth but didn't, or meant to be kind but were rude in spite of our best intentions. I forget at least one significant thing each day and have spent the last week trying to remember the name of those big pink plastic birds with the long spindly legs that people put in their front yards. There are people who really, really don't like me and think that I am too bossy and impatient. And they are right, I can be. I don't wake up in a good mood every day and rarely make it all the way through a twenty-four-hour period without cursing like the truck driver I must have been in a past life. Even so, I'm the best I've got and I wake up every morning grateful to find myself breathing, alert, and willing to face whatever comes. If I lose the car keys, I lose the car keys. If I'm late for a meeting, I'm late for a meeting. All the way through I know that I'm giving everything my best shot and that is where my obligation ends. I'm not better than you, but I'm not worse than you either. Ditto for you. As my friend, Wayne John, says, "We all move our bowels in the same way. And if we didn't we'd all be dead." Ah, the wisdom of that man.

To live a life of joy, moving toward self-acceptance is job number one. It is virtually impossible to feel joy for someone else when you can't feel good about yourself. Sharon Salzberg is one of Western Buddhism's best-known and much-loved teachers. She has been teaching a form of practice called insight meditation for more than twenty-five years. One would expect her to communicate a deep acceptance of herself, which she does. She is also very open about her own struggles with the experience of joy. My favorite story is one she tells of how she has a tendency to berate herself for mistakes. Sound familiar? Sharon knew that self-acceptance was growing by the small clues that would show up in day-to-day events. One happened when she knocked something off a shelf and broke it. Her usual response was to inwardly yell at herself for being so clumsy, and true to form she admonished herself. Only this time she added, "And I love you." And I love you. Try it. See it as a moral obligation brought to you by all the world's religious teachers.

> *There once was a pearl for sale at an auction. Because its price was so high no one bought it. So it bought itself. Buy yourself. Love yourself and you'll take better care of you and start to feel the protection of the dharma—of your spiritual practice—kicking in.*

And while we're at it, let's lighten up. Joy is light. Yes, there are problems to face and yes, when one considers all the violence, greed, and delusion, not to mention the environmental corrosion around us, the sane response is to weep. And we do. But remember, if we weep at all the great shared tragedies, then we don't need to waste any energy on the minor discomforts that show up every day. When something disappointing happens we can feel disappointed and move on. If we are hurt, we can just be with the hurt, and move on, always reminding ourselves that twenty years from now, whatever it is that hurts either won't matter or will be a poignant memory. We feel. We move on. Life is what it is. Knowing that lightens our hearts, and gives us the freedom to flex our creativity muscles so we can try an array of new reactions to the situations of our lives which will keep coming up until we work through them anyway. And we can stay connected with the emerging set of spiritual friends that has somehow surfaced when we weren't looking. And we feel joy—in spite of all the dreck—we feel joy.

With self-acceptance our stumbling quickens. In fact, you may actually start to feel a sense of urgency to share this joyfulness you've discovered. In the diary of Maura "Soshin" O'Halloran, a twenty-six-year-old Irish American woman who lived in a small Buddhist monastery in Japan in the 1980s, she wrote about this feeling in her diary quite often. Having tasted enlightenment, she wrote about how much she wanted to deepen her practice, and to work harder, not just for herself but for everyone she could, so they would know joy as well.

Buddha taught, Rumi taught, Mohammed taught, and Jesus taught, that there are four very powerful states of consciousness that are worth cultivating for both our own sakes and the sake of the world. Once we have tasted joy, we can open up each one, using them as swords to slash through the barriers between all of our hearts. The first is loving kindness. The second, compassion or empathetic loving kindness, is the utter lack of separation between us, and the knowing that whatever impacts you also impacts me, and vice versa.

Equanimity, number three, means keeping our calm. I always picture surfing when I think of equanimity—not that I was any good when I was moving through my own beach bunny, surfer girl years. I remember how amazing it felt to be standing still on a surfboard even though there was this rush of ocean pushing me, with all of its strength, toward the shore. With small waves, I stood still. With large waves, I stood still. It often felt like I was moving in slow motion. Whatever the size of the wave, and they got bigger than six feet too often for my liking, the sense of stillness was always the same.

Equanimity continues to bring a sense of stillness to me now. When my car's brakes go out, I search for a rosary in my purse, knowing it will be hard to go from seventy-five miles per hour (Michigan drivers' average highway speed) to stop without slamming into someone or something. Underneath—calm, equanimity. The car finds a safe place to stop. Nobody is hit. I win a Benjamin Franklin award for a little humor book I wrote as a catharsis. Momentary pleasure—not a big deal—equanimity. My best friend tells me she has breast cancer. We sob and sob together. We wail. Yet, underneath it, equanimity. These are simply the waves of my life coming and going, giving me fodder for the grist mill of my practice. And I am deeply grateful.

The fourth state of consciousness is sympathetic joy. Buddha called it "the mind deliverance of gladness." What he meant was that this particular form of happiness has the ability to bring us a longer, more deeply abiding joy than we could ever believe possible. He was right, of course. We can each remember moments when we have been deeply moved by someone else's good fortune. They were accepted at the college they wanted so badly; she got the raise; he said yes to the offer of marriage.

Unfortunately, in the competitive society where we now reside, the odds of experiencing these four types of consciousness on a steady basis is not great. This is partly because each of us is taught, at increasingly early ages, to compete to win, no matter what. Someone else's gain is our loss. In school our history books only teach us to revere the first person to accomplish a feat. Who was the second woman to fly solo across the Atlantic? Who performed the second heart transplant? Who was the second person to run the four-minute mile? Losing is for losers, we are taught; to be happy that someone else won is to be stupid. I've seen eight-year-old kids losing a baseball game spit on their hands before they shake hands with the winners at the game's end—the whole team. Their coach taught them how.

We are taught to compete for everything. Each one of us knows at least one story of a best friend stealing a love interest. Some of us are those best friends. Then there are all those tee shirts, the ones that are apparently high fashion in some parts, which exhort us to "Play hard or don't play," which shout, "There is only winning." It sort of makes it hard to be calm, loving, compassionate, and happy for someone else's good fortune.

Yet we must if we are to grow spiritually. Here is a secret to keep you motivated: We can't realize enlightenment alone. The whole world has to come with us. I can't beat you to some imaginary goalpost out in the heavens somewhere. We have to win together, *because we are in this together, you and I.*

Loving kindness, compassion, equanimity, and sympathetic joy help us to remember this truth. When we live in these states of consciousness our journey together can be a happy one. Experience teaches that the feeling of warmth and goodwill that we get when we are honestly happy about someone else's good fortune, is worth whatever labels we are given as a consequence. I've learned to sort of enjoy the sound of "loser." It has a nice ring to it. The word I would choose is *mudita*. We are mudita. In Pali, mudita means to simply have a sense of gladness about us—whatever comes—whatever goes. Buddha taught that this feeling of gladness is a powerful liberator. It frees us from our ego, our need to win, to take over a people, to disparage another race. It's the opposite of dwelling on the negative aspects of our lives: a nonsupportive mate, a lecture from someone else, or scoldings of every shape and size. Promises not kept. (My favorite: "I'll call you.") And all the judging that goes on: some marriages I've seen are a constant stream of judgment and nothing more. If the judgments stopped there would be no marriage. We want everyone to be exactly the way we want them to be, to eat what we want them to eat, to work the way we want them to work—and they want the same thing from us. Go figure.

Such negativity causes us to contract, to pull into ourselves. Some of us walk away from long-term relationships because we are so beaten down by judgment that we just can't take any more. Some of us pull back into our homes like turtles into their shells, spending our days in front of fantasy boxes—televisions and computer screens. Some of us become addicted to our computers and the Internet, knowing that we can log off at the slightest twinge of discomfort. However, in so doing we limit our lives and we limit our potential to spiritually grow alongside others. We strangle all of our emotions in an effort to get away from the painful ones.

Mudita is the neutralizer. It cracks through the wall of judgment, teaching us to be happy for others—whatever their life choices. They have their own road. Mudita—sympathetic joy. There are so many ways to share joy. Yesterday I went to throw a piece of gum away in a trash can and, looking down, saw a fresh bouquet of flowers still in its wrapping, all daisies. I looked around to see if someone had accidentally tossed it in the can but nobody was in sight. So I picked it out of the can, wondering if this is how bag ladies get started. No matter. I took it back to the office I was working in and had a glorious day writing with a fresh bouquet of daisies to keep me company. At the end of the day, knowing that I wouldn't be back for awhile, I gave the bouquet to a woman who, for all the years I've known her, has quietly gone about her business with a ready smile and kind words for anyone who stops to say hello. She was happy. I was happy. Now it's all I can do not to look in that garbage can every time I walk past it.

Someone sends me a book out of the blue. They read it and liked it and are passing it on. My friend David gives me some of his old flannel shirts. Random acts of kindness, of course, are the best. Paying someone else's toll. Quietly cleaning the trash off the corner during an early morning walk. Leaving a bag of toiletries for a homeless shelter. Or a quilt. Paying someone's tuition to a class they've always wanted to take. Leaving Christmas toys on someone's porch. I don't have to give you ideas. You already know what you can do, so get out there and have some fun with this. When you do you will be cultivating gladness, cultivating sympathetic joy. And if you stop and are very quiet in the middle of such activity, you might feel your heart opening and waves of happiness come over you. They may last only seconds, but when they happen you'll know you're stumbling along just fine.

Even in the worst circumstances, acting out of one of these four states of consciousness can have an enormous impact. There is a story that survivors of the holocaust tell. It is about a man named Robert Desnos. One day he was told to climb onto the bed of a large truck with a crowd of other prisoners. The truck was headed to the gas chambers. All the prisoners knew that was their destination. When the truck arrived at the gas chamber no one could speak. Even the guards were silent. Suddenly there was a noise and Desnos jumped up and grabbed one of the prisoners. He told him to show him his palm so he could read it. Everyone was stunned. He looked carefully at the palm. "Oh," he said. "I see you have a very long lifeline, and there will be three children!" He was excited and his excitement was contagious. First one person, then another, offered his hand, and over and over the prediction was of longevity and children. As Desnos read the palms even the guards began to relax, so disoriented by this burst of positive emotion that they were simply unable to push the crowd into the chambers. Instead all the prisoners were packed back into the trucks and returned to the barracks, their lives saved. Some survived the war.

So live in joy, in love, even among the grinches of the world. Live in joy and in health. Let go of winning and losing. Let go of the need to judge, to insist that everyone we know should behave exactly as we want them to behave. Let go of comparisons. Buddha called this "conceit." We don't need to know who we are relative to everyone else. They have their own paths and their paths aren't yours.

Look at prejudice with clear eyes so that can go too. My training as a dharma teacher directs me to have feelings of compassion and loving kindness toward people with whom I am having difficulties. For years I couldn't do it. For me, thinking kind thoughts was like saying I'm sorry to someone who had just beaten me bloody. Much to my amazement, my views have changed drastically over the years. With practice I've come to understand that feeling loving kindness for a difficult person frees me from wasting precious moments plotting how to get even. And I know that people who make others' lives difficult are themselves deeply unhappy. So I can, at last, feel compassion. Please don't get me wrong here. I'm not interested in being friends with someone who is hugely difficult. But I have learned how to share the town we live in and how to let go of reacting to their behavior.

In most of the team-building work I do, I try to begin the process by asking the group if they want to develop some ground rules for how they will interact with each other. As you might guess, people want them. Allowing each person to talk without interruptions is usually the first one that comes up. And invariably someone asks for a ground rule that prohibits demeaning each other. In consultant-speak this is called "mounting behavior." We are all tired of being put down. Demeaning words and behavior become hurtful very quickly and make it difficult for the person who has been the brunt of the behavior to feel positive about the person who has delivered the blows. Demeaning behavior is bullying.

Stopping ourselves from put-downs and other forms of mounting behavior is incredibly hard since most of us were raised in environments where mounting behavior is the norm. By the time we reach our thirties, it's automatic. I still blurt out sarcasms when I'm not paying attention, and when I do, I've learned to immediately say I'm sorry and that I'm working hard to let go of a lifetime habit which has me by the ovaries. Then I take some time to just meditate on loving kindness. You can too. Simply breathe in slowly, and then breathe out the thought "loving kindness," visualizing it spreading upwards to the sky and downwards to the depths. Repeat. Repeat. Repeat until you can feel your whole body mind shift to a calmer, more loving state. Then you can go on with the day a significantly happier person. Don't forget to check the trash cans for flowers.

# Chapter Sixteen

# A Sane Valentine's Day Wish

Before:

---

*With every breath I take*
*I think of you.*
*Where you are.*
*What you are doing.*
*I wonder*
*Do you think of me so much?*
*I need you.*
*I really need you.*
*And*
*I can't imagine life alone.*
*Life without your smile,*
*Your warmth*
*Your body (yes, definitely that)*
*Beside me every night, all night.*
*Happy Valentine's Day.*
*I love you.*

---

After:

_____

*October 29, 1996*

*Dear Wayne John,*

*As I look back on everything we have been through with each other, I can only feel gratitude. That you came into my life makes me smile, just thinking of it. All of our wild Aussie adventures. All the road trips and unending flights over the Pacific. And while I wish we were together, the deepest part of me understands your need for Australia with its wide open sky, long beaches, and big-hearted mates.*

*I miss you. I wish, still, that we could have found a continent where we could both be happy and at home. Most of all I wish you peace and delirious joy and a good woman to keep you company for the second half of your life. (Of course, I'll really be furious if she ends up being a younger, thinner version of me.)*

*I love you forever.*

*Your wife emeritus,*
*Larkin*

_____

Buddha grew up surrounded by pleasure. He had everything he wanted—literally. The best foods, clothes, dancing girls (lots of those), the prettiest girl in all the kingdom as his wife. In fact, his wife was so pretty that he actually abandoned an entire childhood devoid of war games to compete in contests like the ones in King Arthur's time just to prove that he was worthy of her hand. He had servants, a doting set of parents, and a charioteer, Channa, who adored him. He had it all.

Somehow, though, he was not happy. Even though he had access to every imaginable pleasure available, he wasn't satisfied with his life. He wasn't fulfilled. Finally he realized, when he was exposed to old age, sickness, and death as an adult, that all the pleasures of the world could do nothing to protect him from suffering: "Whilst I had such power and good fortune, yet I thought: When an untaught, ordinary man, who is subject to aging, not safe from aging, sees another who is aged, he is shocked, humiliated and disgusted; for he forgets that he himself is no exception. But I too am subject to aging, not safe from aging, and so it cannot befit me to be shocked, humiliated, and disgusted on seeing another who is aged. When I considered this, the vanity of youth entirely left me." (*The Life of the Buddha According to the Pali Canon*, translation by Bikkhu Nanamoli, Buddhist Publication Society, Kandy, Sri Lanka, 1992, p. 9)

On the other hand, Buddha knew how deeply we are drawn to pleasure because he was. And how much that drive gets in our spiritual way, not to mention living sane lives. Anyone who has tasted obsession knows how quickly you can lose your life to pleasure. I think if I added up all the minutes of my life I have used fantasizing about a mate or potential mate and then subtracted those minutes from my age, I'd be at least ten years younger. A quarter of my life gone to pleasure and with what to show for it? Some great anguished journal entries, maybe. But that's about it because pleasure, and hunting for it, yanks us right off our spiritual path. It distracts us unmercifully and can wound us deeply.

Some of the first stories Buddha told were about the damage done by pleasure. One of his best-known talks was about trying to light a fire with a piece of wet sappy wood. Obviously it is impossible to do. We're that piece of wood when we are driven by sensual desires, by the thirst and fever that is lust. We are too soggy to light anything, starting with our own hearts. From a Buddhist perspective, if we are overcome by the need for pleasure we can't disassociate ourselves enough to be able to sit quietly or think straight. "So too, while (one lives) still bodily and mentally not withdrawn from sensual desires, and while his lust, affection, passion, thirst, and fever for sensual desires are still not quite abandoned and quieted within him, then whether he feels painful, racking, piercing feelings imposed by striving, or whether he does not, he is in either case incapable of knowledge and vision and supreme enlightenment." *(The Life of Buddha,* p. 17)

This is not to say that any of us has it easy when we realize that it's time to turn down the fires of desire. Buddha really had a tough time with this himself. When he decided, at age twenty-nine, to abandon everything in his life except his quest for understanding why we have to suffer in our lives, it was sensual pleasure that apparently gave him the most trouble. Even though he was able to meditate, and to concentrate on his meditation better than anyone else, the lure of pleasure remained a formidable hook. He actually started out with two teachers before he finally went off on his own. With the first, Alara Kalama, he was able to achieve a deep level of meditation. Still, Buddha left because Kalama's teachings did nothing to help him move past feelings of lust and sensual pleasure. So he moved on to a second teacher, Uddaka Ramaputta, who coached him in further deepening his spiritual practice. With his help Buddha was able to reach a depth of concentrated practice where there was neither perception nor nonperception. Uddaka was so impressed that he offered him the sole leadership of Uddaka's entire religious community. But Buddha refused the offer, recognizing that sensual pleasure still had a hold on him.

When Buddha later talked about his experiences as a student of the two teachers, he shared with his followers his surprise and disappointment that he couldn't get past pleasure with the help of either of the men. So he had to go on alone. For years he meditated by himself, watching, waiting for understanding. And even on the night of his enlightenment he still struggled, until finally, after six years of searching, he experienced the sensation of freedom from the tethers of all pleasures, awake at last. And with his enlightenment he learned two things that are important to remember: The first is how difficult it can be to let go of our yearning for pleasure. The second is that we can do it, that we each have it in us to let go of the yearning.

Still, it's harder for you and me. We are each a member of a society which pushes pleasure at us constantly. Try turning on the radio and finding a song which isn't about yearning, about desire. It's all pervasive. Proof is in the songs that fill our thoughts, the books that line our shelves, the magazines we reach for. I just received a book titled, *Cheatin Hearts, Broken Dreams and Stomped-on Love: The All-Time Funniest Country Music Titles.* It says it all. Try finding an adult movie where there isn't desire. Try finding a bestselling novel which doesn't include sex or a yearning for sensual things.

Please don't misunderstand: sex is enjoyable. So are other pleasurable things. It's the neediness, the feeling that we aren't living a full life if we aren't having sex, that sidetracks us. It's the feeling that we've somehow failed in life if we aren't mated that drives us to drink, or drugs, or suicide. We have become a society where our success as adults is measured not just by our income or our collection of grown-up toys, but by whether or not we have great sex on average twice a week. If it's once a month, we think we've failed somehow. If it's once a year we're weird (and very happy on that day I imagine). If we're celibate something must be really, really wrong with us. If we don't go out to restaurants we're strange. Don't drink? Must have a problem with alcohol. It doesn't even occur to most of us that we can actually choose *not* to yearn for something or someone.

The addiction to pleasure is what gets in our spiritual way. It's a big boulder and the neediness that is a part of the addiction only makes the yearning more excruciating. Valentine's Day always reminds me of how deeply we've fallen into this pit. Anyone who has ever worked in an office on Valentine's Day knows what I'm talking about.

We all watch to see who gets flowers...and who doesn't. Who gets roses—the one who gets two dozen wins. And those of us, men and women, who don't get flowers or don't give flowers are left out of the game. Outcasts. Rejected. Because our lives aren't chock-full of obvious sensual pleasures. Because we don't have a lover who openly professes his or her love for all the world to see.

I once, single-handedly, destroyed a relationship over this very issue. At the time, I was in love with a very sweet man from Indianapolis (he has since married a woman far too young for him and is raising a second family from scratch). He was always doing kind things for me, mostly out of necessity. I had just purchased my first house, a fixer-upper, and it was literally falling down around me. At the time we were seeing each other, the entire west wall had detached from the rest of the house (I could check the weather by looking through huge cracks), which meant that he would drive to Ann Arbor from Indianapolis to spend weekends with me, rebuilding the structure. It was hard work. He even got a hernia from it, but he kept coming anyway—until Valentine's Day. I waited for some romantic gift to show up. The afternoon passed. Nothing. Evening came. Still nothing. By eight I was livid. Storming out, I drove to the nearest drug store, bought myself the last Valentine's card they had (I had given him a poem that morning) and signed it to me from him. I then went home and read him the card from him to me, and in my most righteous tone, lectured him on what I needed for us to go on. It cost me the relationship. I deserved it.

Our addiction to pleasure is so strong that if we don't get stroked on Valentine's Day or our birthday or our anniversary, we are furious. In my own painful lesson I had built a "love relationship" on unspoken expectations. But it didn't matter to me. If he couldn't read my mind, what kind of a man was he? I see men doing the same things to women. Of course she'll be an excellent cook (and can skin a deer, clean a fish, etc.). And I see the same patterns in homosexual relationships. If you really loved me, we say to ourselves, you would do what I want, and we want everything from the complete control of every decision facing our mates, to sex on demand—and then some.

Then we get mean if we don't get all this pleasure that we have come to expect. The verbal attacks I hear between couples never cease to amaze me in their cruelty. They almost always start with, "If you really...." If you really loved me you would go on this trip. If you really loved me we would have more sex. The fights that grow out of such statements can get vicious. They spiral into separations, into the complete breakdown of the relationship. They push us all toward therapists, or many of us end up with headaches or stomachaches or fifty extra pounds on our bodies.

We mistake our yearning for pleasure for what we really want—peace, happiness, meaning, and contentment. It's hard to know this truth when we are constantly exposed to sex, pleasure, and the illusion of romantic love everywhere we turn. Romantic love is just that.

Romantic. It's not real. It's fantasy and illusion. Its half-life seems to be around six weeks. For six weeks or so (although if you are really good at this you can stretch this phase out for three months), the person we are focused on is perfect. Absolutely perfect. They are what we have been searching for all of our lives, the person we visualized in our soul mate class, the person we've described to our friends, the person who fills the hole in our heart. We can't imagine life without her/him. We are sick with longing. We can't sleep. We can't eat. Whole days go by when we think of nothing else. Weeks go by, then somewhere around month two we start to notice things. He really does snore and I'm not getting enough sleep. She'll be fat like her mother. She talks with food in her mouth. He blows his nose on his shirt. He is never on time. She is always running to the bank machine for cash. I hate cats and he has a cat. Then the real set-up: He'd give it away if he really loved me.

Romantic love sets us up. It's the pot of gold at the end of a rainbow that doesn't exist. As long as we keep looking for it, we'll continue to be disappointed because real love is not about what hoops others have to go through to prove their undying love for us. Real love is something completely different. It is the acceptance of everything that is the other person, whether we stay in the relationship or not.

In Buddhism we are taught that real love is loving kindness and compassion. This is a love that doesn't have conditions. And the purpose of a relationship is simply this: to practice love. A relationship is about taking care of each other, about supporting each other's unfoldment, about being there. And yes, there is sex if you are lucky. But it's not addictive sex, it's celebratory sex. It's thank-you-for-being-you sex. It's let's-get-some-great-exercise-together sex. It's massage sex. It's divine sex. It's a part of a relationship, not what defines the relationship.

How can you shift gears? How can you shift from romantic, addicted yearning, to true love? In his book *Touching Peace*, the Vietnamese monk Thich Nhat Hanh teaches that love is really about the practice of mindfulness (paying attention). Our compassion for someone else comes through our mindfulness. When a couple planning a wedding approach Thich Nhat Hanh, he asks them to consider spending a period of time "looking deeply" at themselves to really understand all the potential joys and sorrows within themselves. What are the beautiful things they will bring into the relationship? What is the compost? The couple is advised to spend an entire year really thinking about themselves and understanding what they have to offer their potential mate. At the end of the year they are considered to be qualified to make a true commitment to the relationship. Some of us need more than a year. And some of us can't do it without therapy. Without mindfulness, this paying attention, our chances of a genuine relationship are slim.

In Buddhism there is an expression, *samyojana*, which means internal knots. We all have them. As a result of being treated unkindly by someone else, an internal knot forms. It might be a knot of anger. It might be a knot of disappointment. We might feel insulted—that is a knot. These knots need to be untied in order for us to be open to a relationship. And the longer they last, the tighter they get, and the harder they are to unravel.

If you catch them early, and deal with them, they can be unwound. Unfortunately most of us don't, so they grow, tighten, and bury themselves, only to later create real problems for us when we are trying to love someone else. So you need to take time to allow the knots to show themselves. Quiet meditation does this best. Through meditation you can untie them, readying yourself for genuine love.

As your meditation muscles grow, you will automatically become more mindful in how you live your life. You will become compassion filled, learning how every day is chock-full of beauty and ugliness. And you will learn to embrace both. And as you do it's like an internal gear shifts. Your emotions stop revolving around pleasure and start revolving around loving kindness, compassion, equanimity, sympathetic joy. Assuming that Valentine's Day is not going anywhere (who am I to take on industries that provide jobs to thousands and thousands of people?), I vote we shift it to a day which celebrates a deep acceptance of each other. We see and accept that we all have internalized joys and sorrows. Over time, our acceptance and understanding of each other will transform into a deep abiding love and loyalty, to each other, and in particular, to our mate. She becomes a precious flower. He becomes a precious flower. If she is watered and fed, she will blossom. If he has warmth and nutrients he will become breathtakingly beautiful. Then, finally, we can sit down, hold our partner's hand, look deeply at him, and say, "Darling, do I understand you enough? Do I water your seeds of suffering? Do I water your seeds of joy? Please tell me how I can love you better."

Compassion is what drives real love. It shows itself as loving speech. It is when we congratulate someone for a job well done. It is when we express appreciation. It is a note telling her all the things of beauty we see in her. It is the surprise letter that thanks him for all the sacrifices he has made for us. It is the avoidance of destructive behavior, whether it is a put-down, a shove, or another manifestation of anger and rejection.

We'll never fully understand each other, of that I am certain. At best we can only accept and appreciate. As we do, our love will grow, our appreciation will deepen, and we will become better listeners. As our appreciation grows, and our obsession fades, we are thrilled at the best friend that has emerged. Conditions fall away, a community of two forms, and through our love for each other we learn to express our love of all that is around us. In our loving, all the world's seeds get watered.

A final word. When in doubt remember this: Our love should bring peace and happiness to the ones we love. If it does not, it is not love.

# Chapter Seventeen

# When All You Still Think About Is Sex

*With the fading away of ignorance
and the arising of true knowledge
he no longer clings to sensual pleasures...
When he does not cling, he is agitated.
When he is not agitated, he personally attains
Nibbana (the final deliverance from suffering)*

— *(The Middle Length Discourses of the Buddha,*
   translated by Bhikkhu Nanamoli and Bhikku Bodhi,
   Wisdom Publications, Boston, 1995, p. 163.)

**Crazy Things We've Done When All We Could Think About
Was Sex with a Certain Someone:**

Notes from a totally nonrandom collection of stories and interviews:

1. Sat in front of her house in my car for three weeks from six AM until midnight.

2. I pretended I didn't understand French so he would keep coming to my house to tutor me.

3. She kept leaving messages on my answering machine that she would blow up my Jaguar if I kept seeing Suzanne...the only problem was that she had the wrong number.

4. I left flowers on her car every day and finally lost my job because it made me late for work all the time.

5. I quit my job and moved to Portland because that's where he lived.

6. I stopped eating. I couldn't do anything because all I could think about was him. Finally I had to be fed intravenously.

7. I walked thirty miles to be with her except I read the map wrong so I ended up in the wrong town.

8. I blew a whole retreat thinking about what sex with him would be like. Five days lost. The only five days I had off from work that year.

9. I killed my teacher's husband so I could be with her.

10. When I was in high school I had this incredible crush on this gorgeous surfer named Phil. I only saw him at the train station on my way to Loreto. I used to find excuses to be at the station for hours at a time in the hope that I would see him again.

11. I later found out that Phil had been doing the same thing. But by then I had moved away. I was brokenhearted for a whole year.

12. B. moved from the Midwest to the East Coast so he could live within a hundred miles of a woman he was in love with. It didn't matter that she was married and pregnant. She might call.

13. Child molesters talk about how their sexual desire for a child is so strong that it overwhelms all reason.

14. C. fell in love with his children's babysitter. He started hitting his wife because she didn't meet his behavioral standards and then moved with the children and the babysitter halfway across the country.

15. I spent seven thousand dollars on cards and flowers for her last year.

16. I sold my car to buy her a necklace she wanted. Now I don't have any way to get to work.

17. She wants to have his baby. That she is in eighth grade she finds unimportant.

18. He has fallen in love for the first time in his life at forty-two years of age. Until now he has been a monk working with families in a small village on a peninsula in Southeast Asia. She is nineteen and

he can tell that she desires him as well. He decides to burn himself to death to protect them both from sexual desire.

19. She can't have him so she drives herself in her car off a cliff, leaving two small children behind.

20. He can't have him so he gets high and has anonymous sex for weeks to get him out of his system. Six years later he is dead.

21. Their parents say they are too young to be a couple so they sit in his car in his father's garage with the motor running until the exhaust kills them.

22. He liked long hair. So I grew my hair. He prefers blondes. So I dyed my hair blond. He likes young women. I just had a face lift. (She is thirty-five.)

Ah, sex. For many of us, maybe most of us, sex is the deepest attachment we have. It has many faces. Some of us are utterly aroused by power. Fame can be a full-body orgasm. For most of us, however, sheer lust is the desire we wrestle with the most. It's a mega boulder on our spiritual path. The Buddhist expression *Mara* describes the hell our obsession puts us through. In Pali, it literally means "murder or destruction," and symbolizes those passions that can overwhelm us, hindering wholesome behaviors and progress on the path to enlightenment.

No one is safe. In Buddha's own story Mara followed him through his whole search for spiritual understanding. Just prior to his enlightenment Buddha had been able to let go of everything—his family, his need for fame or power, his need of thoughts, even his senses...mostly. At that point Mara hit him and he hit hard. He wanted to kick Buddha right off the track. What he used was sexual desire: Lust. Even though Buddha had made it through all the other barriers, the yearning for sex was so deep that it was the last hook Mara had. According to legend, Mara was determined to prevent Buddha from discovering a path out of human suffering. So he first called up a horde of demons to frighten Buddha. No reaction. So Mara pulled out his last and best weapon, his most beautiful daughter. In the last hours before enlightenment she was sent out to seduce Buddha. Fortunately for us she was not successful. My guess is that it was close.

Others were not so lucky. Buddha's personal attendant Ananda, his cousin, suffered deeply from the obsession of a young beautiful woman. At the time Ananda was renowned for his memory; he could remember each of Buddha's talks, word for word. As a result the other monks and nuns kept close track of him, especially if they had missed one of Buddha's talks and wanted to hear what he had said. One day Ananda didn't return from his begging rounds. Buddha sent one of the other monks to look for him and when they returned they had two women with them.

Ananda explained. Several weeks earlier he had stopped by a well for a drink. There he found Prakriti, a beautiful young woman, lifting a bucket of water from the well. He asked her for a drink but she refused because she was an "untouchable" and didn't want to pollute him. His response was to say that he would be happy to have a drink from her. Oh, the impact of a few kind words. Prakriti fell in love right then and there. She couldn't sleep after that. Every thought was of Ananda. She waited by the well every day hoping she'd see him. Twice she talked him into sharing a meal with her and her mother at home. After the second visit Ananda had declined any more invitations since he sensed that she had fallen in love.

Prakriti was obsessed with him, and with sexual desire. She got thinner and thinner and paler and paler. Finally she turned to her mother for help, saying that she wanted Ananda to give up being a monk so he could marry her. She would rather die than live a life without him. Afraid for her daughter's life, the mother prepared an aphrodisiac which Prakriti could use to help Ananda fall in love with her. When it was ready Prakriti went out to find Ananda to ask him to share one last meal at her house. Ananda accepted, thinking he could teach the young woman and her mother enough of the teachings of the Buddha for them to understand the need for Prakriti to leave him alone. Before he could say anything he took a drink of tea and felt his head start to swim and his limbs go limp. He couldn't move. So he sat until the other monks found him. When they did they escorted the three back to where Buddha was sitting. When he asked Prakriti why she had drugged Ananda she replied that she loved him with all her heart and wanted him as her husband, that she could not bear to not have him.

Desire—it had caused her to do things she later deeply regretted.

I was drugged—twice actually. Both were so someone could have sex with me after I had declined a more open offer. The first time it was a friend of my father's. He was very wealthy, very handsome. Who would have guessed? He lived in London in a high-rent district. I remember it was somewhere near Jackie Onassis's apartment. I was nineteen and had gone to London to stay for a few days on my way to France. My father's friend offered me a guest room. On the first night I thought something might be wrong with the picture when he kissed me good night on the mouth. I was shocked because he had a mistress who lived down the street and my nineteen-year-old mind saw them as the perfect couple. On the second night he tried to come into my room. When I confronted him about it the next morning he apologized and told me how deeply attracted he was to me physically.

I thought he was funny, which tells you how naive I was. In my best, I-am-the-princess-of-the-world voice, I remember telling him that if he touched me I would tell my father. His response? A second apology and a promise of hands off. To make amends he offered to take me to his club for dinner. I accepted. When we got there and were seated I excused myself to go to the bathroom. When I returned I sat down, took a sip of wine and suddenly my head started to spin. I was so dizzy I couldn't focus. I couldn't lift my arms. Finally, after what seemed like an hour, I asked him to take me back to the house because I was sick. When he went to get the car, a Rolls Royce, our waiter came up to me and told me he had "slipped a mickey" into my glass and offered to call the police. Although I declined, I did demand to be dropped off at a hotel. Confronting the man later, when I went to collect my belongings, his response was that he couldn't get me out of his mind and he wanted me more than he had ever wanted anything. Over and over he kept saying that we were meant to be lovers and that I could have anything I wanted if I would just stay. He even asked me to marry him. We had known each other for four days.

When all we think about is sex, insanity rules. Greed has won, delusion has won, and Mara owns us. None of us are immune. We *all* have fantasies. It's when they drive the rest of our existence that we are

171

in trouble. One of the great stories that has been passed down in my own Buddhist community is about a member who was a star pupil of Samu Sunim. People who lived in the temple with him still talk about how he would meditate into the night after everyone had gone to sleep, and then be the first one up the next morning, headed for the meditation hall for more practice when the rest were just getting ready to brush their teeth. He was a hard manual worker, kept the Buddhist precepts with great mindfulness, and studied hard. It was all everyone else could do not to succumb to wild jealousy. Finally, one day he announced that he had to leave. "Why?" they asked. "Because all I think about is sex." He had slammed into a very big boulder on the path.

Buddha warned us over and over and over about desire. Here are words from his fire sermon: "Due to sensuous craving, conditioned through sensuous craving, impelled by sensuous craving, entirely moved by sensuous craving, people break into houses, rob and plunder, pillage whole houses, commit highway robbery, seduce the wives of others. Then the rulers have such people caught and inflict on them various forms of punishment. And thereby they incur death or deadly pain."

When we are this kind of obsessed, our "monkey mind" is in control. The costs are high. As I've lived with sexual desire in myself and others, and as I've watched people's sexual desire turn to obsession, I've learned something that has both surprised and fascinated me. These monkey minds are not happy. There is no joy in the obsessing, only hunger. In Buddhism this is the characteristic of a "hungry ghost," a being with a huge appetite but only a teeny mouth. Satiation is impossible. And the yearning repeats itself over and over, until some part of us cries out "enough." Hopefully we haven't killed ourselves or someone else in the interim.

Spiritual practice has the capacity to pull us out of the mire. Buddha's advice was blunt: "Pull the arrow out." Just pull the arrow of desire right out, no questions asked, no pondering. If part of what you are feeling for someone or something is true compassion or loving kindness, that will still be there when desire is calmed, and a love free of attachment will start to grow. This is the love that we all really want to give and to receive. It is what some call unconditional love.

We want to love each other unconditionally, and we want to be loved unconditionally.

To pull the arrow out you first have to admit to the obsession and face it like the spiritual warrior you have become. *This is the opposite of trying to suppress it.* Leo Tolstoy tells a wonderful story of how this works. One day his older brother told him to stand in a corner until he stopped thinking about a white bear. Although it sounded simple enough, Leo wasn't able to do it. Instead he was consumed with thinking about a white bear. He couldn't suppress his thoughts and the more he tried, the more that bear image flooded his brain. Suppression flat out didn't work.

In the same way, an obsession with sex often grows directly out of our effort to suppress our thinking about sex. The harder we try to talk ourselves out of thinking about it, the stronger the image. You know what I mean. We've all lived through this hell at least once. Our job is to *face* the thoughts, to *welcome* them courteously until they finally give up and go away, a summer storm fading. In this way they are addressed directly, so they can be pulled out, just like the arrow. When his monks were wrestling with desire, instead of handing out instructions to chant louder or pray harder, Buddha told them to meditate on the human body. Choosing a beautiful body was okay, but they had to meditate on every orifice, every body part, until the desire subsided, which invariably happened. Many found that, when they really focused on the body, all desire left—not just the obsession with sex, all desire.

Many psychologists offer similar advice; that we only gain control over our thoughts when we stop suppressing them. Unwelcome thoughts go away when you welcome them. When resistance is gone, desire goes.

In Zen there is a very famous series of pictures called The Ox Herding Pictures which depict the stages we each go through, moving from sexual obsession, or whatever is deluding our minds, toward enlightenment or sanity. They are a visual reminder that we really are capable of shedding whatever is blocking our spiritual growth. Drawn in the twelfth century by a Chinese master, Kakuan, the first is a picture of someone starting to look for something. It represents admitting that an obsession is making us crazy. The words under the picture are, "In the pasture of this world I endlessly push aside the tall grasses in search of the bull. Following unnamed rivers, lost upon the interpenetrating paths of distant mountains, my strength failing and my vitality exhausted, I cannot find the bull."

In the second picture the searcher discovers footprints. This represents the sudden recognition that we haven't thought of _____(your object of obsession goes here)_____ in a while. We start to sense that life without _____ may be livable. The words under the picture? "Along the riverbank under the trees I see his prints. Deep in remote mountains they are found. These traces no more can be hidden than one's nose, looking heavenward." This sense of a first breath of freedom from desire expands as we continue to sit with our desire. We just sit, watching it, feeling how it impacts our bodies, our breathing, our skin. We watch. That's all.

In the third picture, the character sees the bull for the first time: "I hear the song of the nightingale. The sun is warm, the wind is mild, willows are green along the shore, Here no bull can hide!" In deep meditation, unattached, we start to understand how much this desire is just us, and really has so little to do with someone else. Beautiful bodies come and go. We get this deep sense that it is nothing more than our own minds which are making us crazy. We realize that sense perception is only a factor in our obsession. The real culprit is our own mind. We see the bull—in other words, we get a glimpse of our monkey mind from an outsider's perspective. Who is that outsider?

The fourth picture has the character catching the bull, signifying deeper understanding. Our monkey minds are totally responsible for creating this desire in us. We can see that now all too clearly. "I seize him with a terrific struggle. His will is inexhaustible. He charges to the high plateau far above the cloud mists or in an unpenetrable ravine he stands." Our practice shifts to a deeper level. Stumbling improves. It feels a little more like floating. Things start to feel obvious. Energy fills our body. Maybe we even sweat a bit.

In the fifth picture the bull is tamed. "The whip and rope are necessary, else he might stray off down some dusty road. Being well trained, he becomes naturally gentle. Then, unfettered, he obeys his master." In this stage we can feel the sanity that comes from freedom from an obsession with sex. But our minds are still like the bull. Without a sincere effort to "stay clean," we can easily stray off onto some dusty road, into the arms of Mara. Where one thought arises, another will follow. We must be careful. We must pay attention, and be mindful. Fortunately, we know how.

A real spiritual shift can happen here. The little character in the pictures is next seen riding on the back of the bull, playing a flute, happy as a lark. For us, this is the moment when we realize we can relax into ourselves, we can survive desire. This is not to say that our lives will be without desire. Desire will simply no longer drive our lives. We won't be so heartsick when things don't work the way we wish they would. Instead compassion, loving kindness, equanimity, and sympathetic joy will settle in. The words of this ox-herding picture: "Mounting the bull, slowly I return homeward. The voice of my flute intones through the evening. Measuring with hand beats the pulsating harmony, I direct the endless rhythm. Whoever hears this melody will join me."

The hardest struggle is over. The anguish lets us go. We can sing again...not country western tears-in-my-beer songs, but the songs we knew as children—before sex. Happy songs. Silly songs. The songs we used to hum when we lay on our backs on the ground watching clouds go by, picking out shapes. We know that we are no longer capable of being fully obsessed with sex. I cannot describe to you how relieved you will feel. You'll want to hug your spiritual practice, tell your friends, write your parents. You may even want to describe what you've experienced with the person who triggered your desire in the first place.

If you keep practicing, keep your concentration, keep paying attention, your feelings of peace and happiness will deepen as you eventually transcend even your own thoughts. Picture seven: The character sits in meditation with the full moon in sight. The bull is gone. "Astride the bull I reach home. I am serene. The bull too can rest. The dawn has come. In blissful repose, within my thatched dwelling I have abandoned the whip and the rope."

Beyond this, what? Beyond this, the way opens. Your path becomes clear, as though the moon has become your very own flashlight, pointing the way. Your spiritual practice transcends everything else; it *becomes* everything else. Every breath you take is your spiritual work, every thought a clue to teach you where you need to focus your energy. And it's as though the entire world, and everything in the world, has been created just to kick your spiritual butt. And the biggest gift of all came from the object of your desire. The one who made you crazy. The one who led you to fantasize about sex a thousand, a million times a day. The one who put you over the edge, who forced you to take on Mara once and for all. Your very own personalized guardian angel, I'd say. Surprise!

And now, finally, after wobbling and tripping and stumbling and whining and hundreds of side trips, you are on your merry way.

Rejoice!

# Chapter Eighteen

# Embracing Change

*If you determine your course*
*With force or speed,*
*You miss the way of the law.*

*Quietly consider what is right and what is wrong.*
*Receiving all opinions equally,*
*Without haste, wisely,*
*Observe the law.*

—The Dhammapada

The Koreans call prostrations "climbing a mountain in one place." I call it purgatory. Basically a prostration is a deep bow to the ground, forehead on the floor. If you've seen the movie or the play, *The King and I,* you've seen prostrations. After a typical slow motion, whining start, I actually enjoy doing them each morning. They get my blood moving, loosen my joints, and clear my head, reminding me not to take myself too seriously because at the end of my life, my whole body will end up as compost anyway. So it's not a good idea to get too caught up in ego. Practicing Buddhists typically do prostrations or deep bows when they enter a holy place or encounter a spiritual teacher. It is a way of showing respect and gratitude to the tradition we've been lucky enough to discover. I always do prostrations, even if only in the form of a slight bow, whenever I enter any place of worship. It's a way of thanking that community for acting on their yearning for the divine.

A second tradition that has become a part of my morning ritual has been to say phrases of encouragement after every twenty-five prostrations. The first is "Great is the problem of birth and death." In an instant I am reminded that life isn't supposed to be easy and we don't have to pretend that it is. (This is not a license to complain, however.) The phrase also helps me to keep my priorities straight. So rather than read *People* magazine when I eat breakfast, I eat quietly and mindfully, cognizant of all the work it took for that bowl of oatmeal and those raspberry preserves to be sitting on my little table. The phrase reminds me that wealth is not about money, it's about understanding the journey, the lessons we've been given to learn. Wealth is about appreciation. My knees and legs are letting me sink to the ground and then lifting me back up. I have a voice that can say words and a mind that can understand them. These are miracles.

The second phrase of encouragement is "Impermanence surrounds us." Again, this carries a sense of appreciation. Again, it is a reminder that life is short and it is busy teaching us lessons that we need to pay attention to, and that an overwhelming sense of change is the constant theme of our days. Nothing, *nothing* is permanent. My cat is dead. My adorable baby boy morphed into a snarling teenager, who has since morphed into a compassionate young man with the courage to embrace his own path as a spiritual warrior, pulling people up from their own sinkholes of despair and depression as he goes. I can only guess what the next morph will be.

Impermanence surrounds us. Change is the river of our lives, yet we fight for control with everything we've got. This is the relationship I want and these are the rules and don't you dare change. We want to be young forever. Well, we won't be. I have friends who are spending a veritable fortune on retaining the beauty of their youth. Reconstructive surgery, hair dye, nose jobs. While I applaud their tenacity and grin at my own plucking out of gray hairs when I spot them, ours is a losing battle, because change is inevitable. We'll lose our beauty if we haven't already. We'll age and we'll die. Our work will change and our mates will change—sometimes completely. And our children, they will change because life is just that—change. It is impermanence.

By the time I get to the impermanence phrase I'm usually on a real roll. The prostrations are starting to feel like a sort of upside-down aerobics class or power yoga. At the seventy-fifth prostration, the phrase is "Be awake each moment." Don't miss anything. Pay attention. Embrace the truth of each difficulty, however small. Wake up to the whole glorious catastrophe we are living. Notice the knee, hear the bird, smile at the subway technician. Don't miss a single moment of this extraordinary movie which is your life. Even the smallest segment can teach you unfathomable lessons. Not to mention peace, understanding, and even joy in the face of all the storms which come our way.

At the hundredth prostration the phrase is, "Do not waste your life." I promise myself that I'll remember the words, knowing I'll probably "waste" at least a part of my day as long as Rosie O'Donnell has her own talk show and *People* is published. Such is my human condition. Thank goodness I am not closer to any magazine stands or I'd use up even more of my days on all the world's gossip. "Do not waste your life." What is the most important thing you need to be doing right now? Where should you be today? Who should you be with? Life is short, impermanent, and tough. Don't waste it.

Invariably, as I sip tea or slug down a diet soda later in the day, my mind always retraces itself to those four phrases and I am struck by the power of spiritual practice to keep us on track. I realize that all the meditating and the chanting, all the study, and all those prostrations, have been providing the tools we need to truly embrace the reality of each of our lives and to accept change.

Then I think about how much I hate change. I just hate it. I was furious when I had to give up my bottle for cups and not much happier when I had to give up my wildly entertaining preschool years for kindergarten, where there were no coffee breaks. So uncivilized. I was mad whenever we had to move as kids, and it took fifteen years to forgive my parents for getting a divorce, even though it was clearly in everyone's best interest, including mine. I hated substitute teachers and new bosses, and even today dread the ending of a business project because it means my clients will be changing. And it doesn't help to have such frequent political elections either. Just when I'm getting used to the personality traits of one elected official, there's a new one to figure out. I mourn the loss of every single person who leaves our temple, whatever the reason.

It was good to learn that this resistance to change is due to primal brain parts. Lillie Brock and Maryanne Salerno, the owners of Interchange International, an international consulting firm in Washington, D.C., convinced me of this truth. It turns out that we each have at the core of our brains a layer of neural networks that has the job of keeping us alive. A laudable job, don't you think? It tells us when to fuel our bodies with food, when we're thirsty, and when it's a good time to be afraid of something. New data that is a result of something changing in our lives can create havoc. If our experience is of a quick change, such as when we slam the brakes on in the car to miss a squirrel who has decided to play a game of truth or dare with his buddies, we sweat, shake, and flat-out don't like the experience. If we pay attention we'll notice that fear surfaces, and if we have to brake for squirrels on a regular basis we could end up with lots of fear, which often clumps together into one of my favorite expressions of the nineties—chronic anxiety. So this brain layer does not like change and it will do almost anything to fight it. You know the behaviors. We start eating lots of fat again, like a spoonful of peanut butter, and another and another. We go back to an old lover even though she was selfish, mean, and arrogant, and we swore on everything that is sacred to us that we wouldn't. The new job is scary, so we quit. We go back to the neighborhood bar because that's where all our friends are. You know the drill.

On the other hand, spiritual growth, by its very definition, embraces change. And it's change that you and I want or I wouldn't be writing this and you wouldn't be reading it. We want to change. And those of us who have gone into seminaries, or attended retreats, really want it badly. Understanding change becomes critical once our practice has taken hold because it explains why we may still have difficulties in living a fully spiritual life.

Too bad we're up against our own primal brain. It makes this stuff hard. Maybe even harder than anything else we've ever tried before, especially once we start "being spiritual" rather than reading or talking about it. Why? Because real change, moving from a taste test to an honest-to-goodness new habit, never happens at once. We are retraining our cells. And our brain. There are stages and we need to stumble through each one of them for our spiritual lives to take hold.

Happily, there are at least a dozen social scientists who know how to coach us through change. For me, Lillie and Maryanne teach this best. Here's what I've learned from them. Any time we experience change, if we really want it to become a part of how we live each moment, we need to make it through six stages. In the first stage, even with self-inflicted change such as a commitment to meditate each day, our primary experience is one of loss. Even if we want this change we have to give up something to get it. For me, meditating each day meant giving up the morning and evening (there might be something I haven't already heard) news, a twenty-year habit. You may have to give up morning or evening sex (I never promised you a rose garden) or calling your mom every night. The kids may need to dress themselves. You might have to ask your house mate if she can wait an extra twenty minutes in the morning before she blasts the soundtrack to "Phenomenon" through the house.

We need to learn how to work with change if we're ever going to get off this samsaric roller coaster we call life. The first stage can be scary because it's new and because that layer of neural networks has been well trained to tell us that new things are scary.

Stage two is the "What the hell am I doing?" stage. I remember feeling so stupid when I started meditating. I was afraid to tell my friends and terrified that one of my kids would walk into the bedroom to find their mother sitting cross-legged on a pile of pillows staring at the floor. Meditation did not make me noticeably calmer and I resented having one more thing on my "To Do" list every day. And I definitely, most definitely, missed the sex. (see Chapter Seventeen.) There was a ton of doubt in stage two. A parade of "what if this is a setup, some sick joke?" questions cut through everything. There was even a part of me that was irritated that I had even stumbled onto a spiritual path in the first place.

I found excellent excuses not to meditate. The house needed cleaning, so I reorganized all the cupboards in the kitchen a half dozen times. I felt an incredible need to call friends right when I was sitting down to meditate, convincing myself that it was a psychic connection I was feeling, which meant that it must be important. And I was cranky a lot. That was a real surprise. Here I had found something that called to the deepest part of me and it was infuriating me. Lillie told me this is just the "junior high" stage of change. What a relief that was, although she made me cranky too. I didn't leave anyone out.

If you hang in there, stage three unfolds, I promise. Here, the change toward a more active spirituality is just plain uncomfortable. Even if we want the change, anxiety can surface and we start to forget why we started taking our spirituality so seriously in the first place. I was confused. I knew I didn't want to go back to the eye twitch and the hyperactivity. On the other hand, this was unknown territory. Maybe it would make me crazy. I had heard about people in India who had such strong experiences of enlightenment that they wandered for days in a state of bliss, not even remembering their own names. With my luck it would happen to me in Newark, New Jersey's airport and then where would I end up? I pictured myself spending the rest of my life in one of the last insane asylums in the United States, somewhere on Long Island. No one would ever find me, my children would grow up without their mother, and my then husband would surely run off with another woman. It was rough.

Lillie and Maryanne have convinced me that this is the most critical stage in the change cycle because it is when the still primal part of us starts whining that surely things weren't that bad before we started this spiritual thing. The trick is to just keep going. Things do get better. Buddha said the same thing. So did my teacher. Over and over Sunim reminded me to just keep meditating, just keep meditating. When I told him I couldn't concentrate for a half hour he told me to sit for fifteen minutes. When I said that was too much, he suggested five. When people come to me at this stage in their practice, if they can only do a minute of sincere practice, I say a minute will do. That's all. The important thing is to just *keep going.*

When I said I just couldn't sit still because of the discomfort, Sunim told me to do walking meditation. When I whined that even that felt too hard, he told me to take a break and go into the woods where nature would meditate with me and where I could look to the trees and birds for guidance—so I did. And it worked. Finally I was able to move on to the next stage.

Stage four is where we start to have this visceral sense that our new lifestyle will take hold. The signs are subtle. You wake up pleased for the opportunity to meditate or pray. You notice that nobody has interrupted your sitting in the last week. And you've been able to wait to call your friends. Meditation starts to feel just right somehow, like a pair of new shoes that stops giving you blisters. Anxiety disappears, or at least you've faced it so often that it is almost comfortable, like hearing your grandmother admonishing you to stop driving so you won't get in a car accident. You listen, you love her, you go on with your life.

I loved this stage. I could tell I was in it because I needed less sleep and woke up with energy, eager to meet each day. My creativity was in high gear: One day I woke up, and before I was out of my jammies I had designed an entire team-building retreat for a client, using a scavenger hunt as the core activity. Then I wrote all the lyrics for a melody a friend had written and prepared an all-blue dinner (blueberry soup, blueberry muffins, salad with blue cheese...) for the family. I knew it was "tomorrow" and the sun, as Annie promised, had come out. Meditating was a breeze and I looked forward to it always, resistance free.

Two more stages complete the cycle of change. The fifth stage is about energy. You've integrated spirituality into your life. And it's working. You can see shifts taking place in how you view and treat the world and how it treats you back. Confidence surfaces. You know what you're doing. You start talking about your spiritual practice very openly. I recall stage five as the period when I just wanted to talk about spirituality all the time. I started asking friends and colleagues if they wanted to check out some of the spiritual lectures that are a constant part of the Ann Arbor program. I even asked my lover, a die-hard Libertarian/atheist, if he would mind giving me a ride to the temple so I could attend the daily five AM services. For me the feelings of this stage were very similar to a sense of falling in love. I couldn't meditate enough, read enough, chant enough. I was euphoric and could feel my heart swell so full of the experience that sometimes tears of gratitude would stream down my cheeks. It was bizarre. And yes, several people asked me if I had found some excellent drug that I wasn't sharing.

My heart was home and I understood the deep power of the change cycle and how important it had been to see it through.

The sixth and last stage of the cycle is when we fully integrate our spirituality into our every moments. We embrace it fully, unafraid. I can no longer imagine a day without meditating in some form or fashion, walking or sitting. In between other activities I find spaces for prayer. Sometimes it's standing in the line at the bank or sitting in a traffic jam or waiting to see my accountant. Reading spiritual scriptures has pushed Danielle Steele, Clive Cussler, and John Grisham out of my life, except on those transoceanic flights where I will do almost anything to help time fly. And the happiness, the little kid happiness, what a trip! Even during miserable moments, underneath lies a still peace that is happy.

Since impermanence surrounds us, we will always have to face changes. Every day there will be changes. Some will be small, like a new color on the door. Others will be life-size. Some will be spiritual. Some won't. The HIV test is positive, you get an offer of marriage, the venture capital firm says yes. The only way to live with change is to embrace it. It's another dragon that needs staring down.

There are tried and true methods for doing this. When you first get serious about this stumbling stuff and your body and family and friends are first introduced to the emerging you, it is critical to do several things for yourself. Number one is to take good care of your physical self—eat well, get enough sleep, exercise, and definitely have a good bubble bath once in awhile. Number two is to plot out a daily pattern and stick with it. It also helps greatly to simplify your life however you can. You don't have to sell your house but you might want to consider cleaning out things that are crowding you. You know what they are. Some people have cut back on work hours, given up expensive vacations, taught their teenagers to cook the meals. Fake friends can be freed. Unused clothes, furniture, books, and whatever else is crowding you. (For me it was jewelry. Go figure.) can be donated to your favorite nonprofit. Then create a space, even if it is a corner in your bedroom.

That is your official spiritual spot. You can make an altar if you like—a picture, a flower, rocks, a candle or two. This is where you can turn off your monkey mind and meditate, where the world can go on "hold," thank you very much, for a small period each day.

When resistance strikes, go be physical. Sunim suggests prostrations. About a thousand. I'm with him. I haven't found any resistance, particularly in the form of a negative emotion, that prostrations can't cure. It you don't have the four or five hours it would take, then go walk fast or run or dance until your body is covered with sweat. Then you'll be able to sit. The resistance will either be gone or much weaker. If it is still strong, go dance some more, do the prostrations again, or get on your bike. Whatever you do, keep returning to your sacred space for breaks, for prayer, for practice. If you discover a pot of anxiety embedded in your brain, head for nature. A botanical garden or a hiking trail. Take someone camping with you, or do walking meditation. Go volunteer: Ask permission to rock some AIDS babies in the hospital or clean someone's house for them. The main thing about resistance to change is that it is your EGO fighting for its life. If therapy is the only thing you think will help, well then—praise Allah—there are some excellent therapists around. Go find one.

Just don't slide. *Don't slide.* You've come so far. If your practice has taken you to the point where you can see your resentments and fears and how you are sabotaging your spiritual work, you are actually closing in on stage four of the change cycle. Keep going. Read about other people's experiences. Read about spirituality. Try to give your spiritual work more time if you can. And of course, there's always chopping wood. Attitude matters a lot in the change process. Being committed to living a healthier life matters. Discipline. Courage. Humor. In the "Flower Ornament Sutra," a famous collection of Buddhist teachings, there is a passage where someone asks what it takes to become an enlightened being. He asks the question in about nine hundred different ways. The answer given is straightforward. More than anything else, determination is what counts. We need to be determined to find our spiritual path and then to integrate it into how we live our lives. We need to see the change cycle all the way through.

You'll be able to handle whatever comes along, by the way. Whenever I was having a really tough go as a teenager and young adult, my mother used to say to me, "Honey, you can handle this. If you couldn't you would be dead." It always seemed pretty harsh at the time but she was always right. I was always able to handle whatever it was, however awful. You can too. Just keep going. Left foot. Right foot. Left foot. Right foot.

When you learn how to embrace and integrate change, you also discover new ways of understanding what words like love and justice and anger mean. Love becomes loving kindness naturally. And compassion. As anger opens itself up it shows its real face, which is fear, and the deeper the anger, the deeper the fear. Being right where you are and giving whatever is before you the best attention possible. As you do, understanding surfaces, and wisdom. And at a deeper level, real, really real love. All will come courtesy of change.

# Chapter Nineteen

# The Way

*There once was a young fish who went to one of the older fish and asked, "I've always heard about the sea. What is it? Where is it?" The older fish replied, "You live in the sea. And the sea is within you. You are made of sea. You will end in sea. The sea surrounds you as your whole being."*

What do you think?

*A HEARTLAND INTERPRETATION OF SEVERAL VERSES ON THE FAITH MIND BY SENGTSAN (3RD ZEN PATRIARCH):*

*Finding peace isn't hard*
*if you have no opinions.*
*Gushing yes or gushing no need to be absent*
*for clarity.*
*Even a little opinion gets in the way.*
*Even a teensy opinion*
*separates heaven and earth in infinite miles.*

*So.*
*If you really want peace*
*To be happy,*
*Secure*
*Then hold no opinions.*
*None for.*
*None against.*

*The need to categorize everything into*
*What we like or dislike*
*just makes us crazy.*
*(But you already knew that.)*
*When you let your opinions get in your own way*
*so you can't see what is really going on*
*You'll never find peace.*
*What a cost.*
*How unnecessary.*

*The way to truth is like a wide ocean*
*the widest you can possibly imagine*
*and then some.*
*In that ocean nothing is lacking.*
*Nothing is in excess.*
*If it wasn't so painful it would be funny*
*—you know—*
*how our needing to categorize*
*categorize*
*categorize*
*"I accept this"*
*"I reject that"*
*causes our lack of peace.*
*Because we just can't see the true nature of things.*

*To find your way, live neither in the noise of everything*
*that is outside of you*
*nor enslaved by all your inner feelings.*
*Instead find peace in the connection of everything*
*in all of our oneness.*
*And the rest will take care of itself.*
*Even your opinions.*

*This is the irony.*
*If you actively try to stop all your opinions*
*If you try to use the power of your own will*
*—you will fail.*
*Because your very effort just fills you*
*with more opinions.*
*Try it and you will see the truth of this yourself.*

*On the other hand, trying to force yourself*
*to be peaceful*
*is just as painful.*

*Don't obsess.*
*The more you do*
*The more you talk about this*
*think about that*
*The farther you get from peace.*

*So stop talking.*
*And stop thinking.*
*Let peace find you*
*the way it always does*
*when you let it.*
*Let go.*

*Return to your life moment by moment*
*and everything you need*
*will find its way to you.*

*At the moment of peace*
*in that breath of understanding*
*your heart will soar beyond*
*appearances*
*and opinions.*
*And you will realize that everything you think is real*
*only seems to be real because of ignorance of the way.*

*Don't search.*
*No flashlights, strobe lights, candles.*
*Just give up your opinions.*

---

You can let go now. All your dragons have shown their faces. Some might still look like dragons. Others will look like puppies, making you wonder what it was that was so scary. Watching your anger, you see that it comes and it goes. It is weakening from your watching. Creating a space for it in your meditation may have opened up all sorts of creative ideas for facing specific sticky situations head on, weakening their force as well. Quite a roll you're on here. You understand change. You know its cycle and how to monitor your own resistance to each phase. Colors might be brighter, emotions may surface more quickly. You know instantly if it's rage shooting up your spine and when the obsession is sex.

The compost that is our lives is excruciatingly rich. It is filled with our mundane suffering and anxieties which have served as preoccupations for the mind and nothing more. Now is the time to let go, to simply live your life wonderfully entertained by what each moment offers. Now you can follow the way. Your stumbling has been transformed to a calm, gentle walk across time.

After six years of what I can only describe as half-hearted meditation, I finally had my first experience of concentrated practice. The difference was extraordinary. Time stood still. It felt like I was surrounded by a warm gentle space which was, for some weird reason, pleased to be with me. There were no thoughts scanning across my hyperactive brain. I was just sitting. Afterwards, I was struck by how rested I felt. It was like my insides had had a shower or a massage or something. They felt clean. I was clean. And you know what the best part was? I had tasted the freedom—for the first time in my entire life—of no opinions. Not a single judgment had crossed my mind. No categories. No worries. Just sitting. (No, it wasn't better than great sex. Everyone always asks me that. It was different.)

For awhile afterwards I was able to simply live my life, to do what was right in front of me; and to think clearly about any issues that surfaced, and respond with a fair amount of compassion. Today this clarity comes and goes, often depending on how much meditation I've been doing lately. It brings with it a peacefulness that feels a lot like I remember feeling when my mother used to brush my hair when I was very small. This is the way. And if I can get here, anybody can get here. It only takes practice and a willingness to believe that anything is possible.

Samu Sunim talks about faith often. In a recent letter to members of the Toronto Zen Buddhist Temple, he described his experience as a young monk, begging for food in Korea in the 1950s. His teacher told him to look for Buddhas, for people who were perfect teachers for him, while he begged. It was harvest time and his duty was to travel to various farming villages to deliver Kondae, donation bags for rice. Later he would go back to collect the bags, which would be full of rice. Sunim would secretly look for Buddhas while he was accepting the rice donations, but he couldn't find any. When he went back to the abbot to report this, the abbot shouted at him to keep looking, but don't look for special Buddhas. Aha! Buddhas don't have to be special. After that Sunim was able to spot many Buddhas, realizing that each of us is a Buddha when we are our best selves. He realized that it was his own sense of self that had been in the way of finding Buddha in everyone. Once he let go of his self he was able to honor all of us as a Buddha.

Zen Master Huang Po, also known as Hsi Yun, is believed to have died around 850 A.D. He had a habit of teaching hundreds of spiritual travelers at a time, often using metaphors and stories to point to the spiritual path. Sometimes he would compare our minds to the sun as it travels through the sky, sending out light uncontaminated by even the finest particle of dust. Huang Po's dharma talks were strong and his words clear: "Ordinary people do not seek the way but merely indulge in their six senses....A student of the way, by allowing himself a single (sense-driven) thought, falls among devils. If he permits himself a single thought leading to differential perception he falls into heresy....Nothing is born, nothing is destroyed. Away with your dualism, your likes and dislikes. Every single thing is just one mind. When you have perceived this you will have mounted the chariot of the Buddhas."

Now there's a tee shirt: "I have mounted the Chariot of the Buddhas." To win one, you have to keep at your practice. All the great teachers remind us of this whether they are telling us that it's not that we can't do it, but that we don't do it, or it's Yoda admonishing us that there is no "try."

Abbot John Daido Loori teaches at the Zen Mountain Monastery in Mt. Tremper, New York. He often teaches through the use of koans. I love his dharma talks because he pulls the ancient teachings into the present, and he teaches about the way, the path. In one discourse which has since been printed in *Mountain Record*, a journal of the Zen Mountain Monastery, he uses a koan about a river and ocean to point out the way: "The Prologue: The river never speaks, yet it knows how to find its way to the Great Ocean. The mountains have no words, yet the ten thousand things are born here. Where the river finds its way, you can perceive the essence. Where the mountain gives birth to the ten thousand things, you realize the action. When the mind moves, images appear. Even if the mind does not move, this is not yet true freedom. You must first take off the blinders and set down the pack if you are to enter the sacred space. When you let go, even river rocks and brambles are radiant. When you hold on even the Mani jewel loses its brilliance. When you neither let go nor hold on, you are free to ride the clouds and follow the wind.

The Main Case: Buddha has said, "All things are ultimately liberated. They have no abode. Master Dogen says, "We should realize that although they are liberated, without any bonds, all things are abiding in their own Dharma state."

John Daido Loori says, "Our tendency is to just see things from one side or the other and to miss the profound teaching that is neither one side nor the other, that is the place of merging between one side and the other. *When the mind moves, images appear.* We talk to ourselves. We create ideas and concepts. And yet, even if the mind does not move, it's just another nesting place, it's not yet freedom. How do you go beyond those two extremes? *Take off the blinders, set down the pack*—this refers to the stuff we carry, the ideas we hold on to. It's only when you let go of the baggage that you can enter "the sacred space." And where is the sacred space? Right where you stand. But it can't be seen until those blinders are removed and the pack is set down. It is then that even river rocks and brambles are radiant." (John Daido Loori, "The Sacred Teachings of Wildness," Dharma Discourse: Koans of the Way of Reality, Case 108, *Mountain Record*, Winter, 1992, pp. 2-3)

Mountains and rivers are the ups and downs of life. They will always exist. Everything is the way, once we sink into our practice. The whole world becomes our path, and our compost. This discovery means that we have cleared out all the gunk that has been cluttering our minds, we have lightened up, and our spirit has grown. We've learned to listen with our eyes and to see with our ears. This is when we start to understand the teachings. And this is when we hear the sermons of the rocks and the teachings of the mountains.

Thus we find ourselves making a deeper commitment to our spiritual work. This might take the shape of small steps at first. Maybe you discover that you find a way to spend more of your time meditating, and less of your time at parties. Your life becomes quieter. Even the radio gets turned down—or turned off. Some of us become religious about going to church regularly or find ourselves actually paying attention to what is being said and done in the religious services. Generosity becomes more natural. You may start looking for longer retreats; two days or five days just isn't enough. Vacations shift from outer experience to inner work. Our creativity grows. So does our commitment to living a sane life. We may finally decide to join a recovery group to get help with some psychological arrow that we just can't pull out on our own.

Some of us even enter a seminary because, what the heck, it's there.

This is the way. It has ten thousand entrances and they can each be entered in as many ways. If you are still unsure, still stumbling, increase your practice of generosity. Put some muscle into it. Use kind words. Do good work.

It's time to choose.

Dallying is not recommended.

# Chapter Twenty

# Fear, Worry, and Shame

---

### Twelve Steps for Dealing with Misery

1. Get over yourself. You are not the center of the universe.
2. Repeat a hundred times a day: Nobody can read my mind.
3. Stop watching the news. If it's bad enough you'll hear about it.
4. Change jobs.
5. Move.
6. Buy some new clothes from the consignment shop.
7. Shave your head so there will be something new to focus on.
8. Forgive your parents.
9. Repeat number eight for all your former mates.
10. Reintroduce calming music into your life.
11. Babysit someone else's kid. A baby with colic is good.
12. Quit reading your horoscope.

---

We suffer because we grasp and we crave. Even as we move along our path we suffer. Fear is one of the boulders that remains to block our progress. And that feeling of anxiety that surfaces from our fear that there might be something dangerous about this spiritual choice, can stop us cold. For some, shame arises as we think about our own unskillfulness in day-to-day activities, and as we remember the big mistakes we have made getting to here. Shame includes all those excruciating emotions that come from guilt, embarrassment, a feeling of unworthiness or disgrace. Quite a big boulder, shame. Or worry can jump out at us, manifesting as a nagging unease that refuses to go away, even as we give ourselves permission to explore what it means to be spiritual. These can be surprise boulders in our road. "Why now?" we ask ourselves. Because we're getting to the bottom of things. And discovering, much to our collective dismay, that in the end we cling to wanting the world to be exactly the way we choose. I know I do. Even when that is not the problem, when instead we are at the point where we have let go of everything to keep moving, then whack—shame, worry, or fear show up. Maybe all of them at once. And we are pushed off center. This is natural. As our practice deepens, the superficial negative emotions such as irritability rise and fall relatively easily. A good five minutes of meditation and they're history. You just don't get riled any more when someone cuts you off on the highway (unless it's the same guy). Some one else's sarcastic humor doesn't grate the way it used to. Anger arises less frequently, and when it does arise, it doesn't last. But fear, worry, and shame—they are tough. They can make your spiritual efforts take a nose dive. Even though this is just a phase (I promise), it's a rough and tumble one, and getting through it takes real tenacity.

Sometimes I think that these emotions stick to us so tenaciously because we *like* to be miserable in some perverse way. Liesl Schillinger, the mother of recovery programs for dealing with misery, once asked in a *Washington Post* article, when the last time was when any of us heard someone walk into a room talking about how happy and energetic they felt. It's rare. Mostly what we hear is someone (often ourselves) groaning that they're feeling down because of _____ (you fill in the blank). Whining has become a part of our social landscape, and it feeds worry, fear, and shame like dry pine needles feed a fire. We are so proficient at it, and it is so seductive, that only your gut commitment to spiritual growth, your promise to yourself that you are going to keep going no matter what happens, will move you past the boulders. But then, that's the miracle. Your commitment moves you right on through.

One of my biggest shocks as I learned about Buddhism was the discovery that even Buddha experienced negative emotions as his spiritual side matured. Not shame and worry so much, but he was plenty scared. When he left his home in search of enlightenment and met up with Kalama and deepened his meditation to where he had achieved a state of "nothingness," he observed that this ability was not helping to control his emotions. You already know that it did not rid him of lust. It also did not lead to freedom from fear. It wasn't enlightenment. He moved on. Then, with Uddaka, teacher number two, he was able, you'll recall, to deepen his practice to a place where there was neither perception nor nonperception. But even that didn't free him completely from his emotions. It wasn't enlightenment. He moved on.

One day he came upon a delightful grove of trees near a river which seemed to be a good spot to dig in. At first Buddha was really excited. As he thought of other practitioners he figured that they would be filled with fear and worry if they tried to sit alone the way he was planning to do. In his mind, he was different—a noble one, free from such defects. Wrong! He was scared too. Worried. "I dwelt in such awe-inspiring abodes as orchard shrines, woodland shrines, and tree shrines, which make the hair stand up. And while I dwelt there, a deer would approach me, or a peacock would knock off a branch, or the wind would rustle the leaves. Then I thought: 'Surely this is the fear and dread coming." And when he walked into the forest he tried to talk himself out of the fear. He figured he would just subdue it: "Why not subdue that fear and dread while maintaining the posture I am in when it comes to me?" Great idea except that it didn't work. The farther he walked into the forest, the more fear he felt. There were lions, there were tigers, there were noises that he didn't recognize, and it was dark.

In fact, as he prepared to sit, Buddha was overwhelmed with fear and dread. He found that even though he had moved past many emotions and attachments, the toughest ones were still hovering over him, ready to pounce.

These emotions, the ones that cling to the bottom of the barrel, are the threads that keep us connected to our ego, our small self. Think of them as a sort of last ditch effort to blockade our full experience of the divine.

Back to Buddha. He decided to sit them out—to just sit them out. "While I sat the fear and dread came upon me; but I neither walked nor stood nor lay down till I had subdued that fear and dread. While I lay, the fear and dread came upon me; but I neither walked nor stood nor sat till I had subdued that fear and dread."

So he sat under a Pippala tree. And insights flowed as fear dropped away. He saw that each cell of his body was its own universe and utterly connected to a mighty river of birth, life, and death, birth, life, and death. He saw how impermanent our feelings are, how they appear and disappear like bubbles beside a stream. He understood the damage done by our mistaken perceptions of how things are—our struggle to accept that in the end, we are all surrounded by impermanence and we are, ourselves, impermanent. He saw the suffering caused by our mental states. How worry makes us mad, the damage of shame, the monster potential of fear.

These are what comprise the darkness, these mental states are what cause suffering. And finally he understood that the cause of such mental states was a special form of ignorance. We just plain don't understand the deep compassion and joy of the divine, which is our own inherent Buddha nature. In breaking through the ignorance we could free ourselves from the dark. "He smiled and looked up at a Pippala leaf imprinted against the blue sky, its tail blowing back and forth as if calling him. Looking deeply at the leaf, he saw clearly the presence of the sun and stars—without the sun, without light and warmth, the leaf could not exist. This was like this because that was like that. He also saw in the leaf the presence of clouds—without clouds there could be no rain, and without rain the leaf could not be. He saw the earth, time, space, and mind—all were present in the leaf. In fact at that very moment, the entire universe existed in that leaf; the reality of the leaf was a wondrous miracle." (Thich Nhat Hanh, *Old Path White Cloud,* Parallax Press, Berkeley, California, 1991, p. 115)

Buddha did not come to his understanding by thinking. Thinking is simply a manifestation of our ignorance. Instead it was a combination of mindfulness and meditation practice that proved to be the sword capable of slicing through his ego and the last of the negative emotions.

And here you and I sit trying to figure out how to get through our own darkness, wondering what we can do. The teachings are clear. Running away from the emotions never works. Numbing them with alcohol or drugs only postpones dealing with them. And they won't be ignored. If they can't surface as thoughts, they'll surface as some form of phobia, neurosis, or maybe even physical disease. And yet, moving ahead on our path is stalled by their very existence. What can we do?

First, acknowledge them. Accept them. As was true for anger and rage, fear, worry, and shame can not be willed away. They first need to be acknowledged and accepted. Embraced even. One of my fellow dharma teachers, Paramita Nat Needle, teaches students to be their own "Jewish grandmother" whenever these emotions arise. First you pretend that there is a huge virtual blackboard in the space in front of you as you sit in meditation or quiet contemplation. Then, when thoughts arise which are related to these negative emotions, in your very best grandmother voice you say (this can be done in silence if others are around because they will think that you have finally lost it if you try this out loud) "Oh, there's _____. (Label the emotion. Is it worry? Is it fear? Is it shame? Don't tell me, please don't tell me it's still sex. If it is, go back to Chapter Fifteen for all of our sakes!) Anyway, you label it. Then, pretending that the label has velcro on its back, you simply stick it to the blackboard in the sky so you can continue to meditate. This is an exercise that frees up space in your mind and your heart allowing for deeper spiritual work. Also, you can come back later and look at your patterns of thinking. If a certain emotion insists on filling the blackboard, it's time to face it. You can face it alone à la Milarepa or Buddha or you can face it with the help of an effective therapist or a wonderful friend.

Most negative emotions will shrink in the light of such attention. If they don't, then they are probably suggesting that some aspect of how you are living your life needs to change for you to hang in with the rest of us. For example, if you discover, through this exercise, that you are physically afraid of your mate, a good question to ask yourself is whether it is time to do something about it. When Buddha embraced his fear of what might happen as his practice deepened, he discovered that he had no reason to be afraid. As his levels of understanding grew, he did not experience negative mental or physical consequences, so he could keep going.

Most worries, fears, and shame are unfounded. If it turns out that you have a good reason to be afraid, to worry, or to feel shame, do something. Only in cases where a person is imprisoned and has no communication channel outside is this impossible. Even then an imaginative, spiritually grounded mind can often think of something. Face it. Embrace it. With shame, ask yourself if you need to make amends to someone for the shame to be lifted. If the answer is yes, then for heaven's sake, go make amends—without compromise and without hurting anyone further in the process. If there is no need for amends, let go of the shame. There isn't anything you can do about it now anyway. You've seen it. You get it. It's the result of past tense and you, my friend, are present tense. Just let it go.

With worry, you already know from your own life experience that worry has never changed anything. If a person's plane is going to go down, it will go down, whether or not we're sitting here worrying about it. All worry does is give us wrinkles, gray hair, and if we're really good, heart disease. I know. Remember I am an outstanding worrier. Give me a topic—your sister has a lump on her breast—and I can worry a whole new crease in my forehead before you tell me she's okay. My blackboard often fills with worries, sometimes becoming so crowded that I have to grin, it's so hilarious. I've learned to thank all the worries for coming, brush them off the blackboard, and return to whatever it was I was doing before I was so rudely interrupted. Planning all the time, by the way, is worrying, and it's about fear of the unknown. While planning is important if we want to get anything done in our busy lives, if your brain starts to plan when you are trying to meditate or pray, it's worry. If you plan and you replan and then plan the same thing again, you are now a card-carrying member of the fraternity of worry warts.

Another strategy for facing these tough emotions is to decide to trust yourself more than you do right now. Trust your own wisdom. Underneath all that ego gunk we know the right thing to do in any situation. This does not mean that we'll do it, but we know what it is. Why? I don't know. I only know that there is this underlying base of compassionate wisdom that resides in each of our hearts. Spiritual practice frees it. I see it happen all the time.

As the Buddha taught,

> *"Do what you have to do*
> *Resolutely with all your heart.*
> *The traveler who hesitates*
> *Only raises dust on the road."*

What if you aren't sure? What if you read these words but somehow, deep inside, you don't know if you trust yourself? Then there is only one thing to do to prove you can: Take risks. Small ones will do. Expand your zone of comfort. Take risks so you can see that it is possible to trust yourself and that you are—forever—okay. You might take a new route to work. Tell someone you are uncomfortable with their unkind remark. Apologize even though she was wrong. Return a faulty product without anger. The opportunities are endless.

Susan Jeffers, author of *Feel the Fear and Do It Anyway*, has wonderful suggestions for expanding our zone of comfort: initiating a friendship with someone who is higher up in the company; calling someone who intimidates us; getting the root canal work done without tranquilizers.

When we take risks, particularly risks which force us to be public about our values and who we are, a funny thing happens. Actually three things happen: First, we find ourselves taking bigger and bigger risks, until it seems as though we are suddenly making a living in a way that heals ourselves and maybe others—not to mention the earth. Or we find ourselves freed of that obsessive relationship we were certain we would never leave. In other words, lifestyle changes happen for the better. Second, our days of being a victim become numbered. You do not have to be assaulted or raped to be a victim in this society. You do not need to be penniless or in a lopsided relationship. *Any time* you give someone else credit for making you angry or worried or shamed you are a victim because you have given the control of your thoughts to someone else. This type of victimization can be subtle, although it never is to your friends. I just got off the phone with a friend from Chicago. He is in love with a wonderful young woman who obviously has the same feelings toward him. They are both smart, active, very attractive, and compassionate—a match that would serve this world well. Except there is this catch: She has been living with someone for five years who has a history of depression. If she ends the relationship she is afraid of what he might do to himself. He has threatened suicide in the past. So she is contemplating not pursuing a healthy, honest relationship with some-one she really loves so that the man she has been living with won't hurt himself. My friend, trying to be supportive, is sympathetic to her staying, even though it is clearly breaking his heart. Talk about victim behavior. No wonder we only get so far on our path and then whack, those boul-ders come hurling toward us. We need to just let go. Let go of thinking. Let go. Yes, it can hurt. And yes, you'll get past whatever it is. And no, you aren't responsible for how anyone else thinks or even acts once your children are past a certain age. Know that none of these negative emotions has ever helped you in any way. If you must cling to some-thing, cling to compassion, laced with honesty. That's a way through.

Will they go away ever? Probably not. But they'll downsize to their true dimensions so you can move past them. And you'll better under-stand where they come from and why you are dwelling on them. Besides you can handle them, remember? Spiritual practice. It's all yours for the taking. No negative emotion can overwhelm the power of a sincere heart and an honest faith in your own possibilities. It never has, never will.

There once was a young monk who went to his teacher in tears. He blurted out that he was having a terrible experience with his meditation practice. Every time he settled down, took a deep breath, and closed his eyes, all he could see were two dragons fighting each other. One dragon was a deep blue and it was filled with anger and greed and lust. Even its fire was terrifying. It was ferocious, this dragon. The other dragon was just as ferocious. Only the other dragon, pale white, was filled with love, wisdom, and compassion. Its fire was a deep, deep yel-low. The young man was terrified of what would happen. Which dragon would win? He couldn't tell and was afraid to watch them fight, which made him afraid to sit. Could the teacher please give him some advice?

The teacher smiled. He looked at his student, his eyes filled with compassion. "Do you want to know which dragon will win?" The young monk nodded. "Why the one filled with love and compassion and wisdom, of course." But how did he know asked the young monk. "Because that's the one you'll feed."

If we feed our fear, worrying, and shame, they grow. They grow and grow until they are dragons that rule our lives. Your job is simply to thank them for visiting and to let them go as best you can, whether its velcroing them to your virtual blackboards or just letting them float on by. Let them go so you can go on with your life. You may need to shift your path slightly if you've learned something useful from their visit, but mostly your job is to let go.

Letting go is a critical life skill, and for most of us it is a learned skill. We don't seem to do it naturally. Several weeks ago I received a phone call from a good friend who told me that she had organized a party for me and another woman we both know well but whom I have great difficulties being around. In my mind, she is a user of people. She seduces people and then gets them to do favors for her until she finds a better deal and then off she goes. When I heard her name I was instantly angry, remembering how I had allowed her to take advantage of me years ago. Noticing myself, I laughed out loud. The weeds of the negative emotions are so deep. Reminding myself to let go, I chanted for her happiness, had a cup of cocoa, and let go of the negative memory, replacing it with positive ones. (I think. The test will be the next mention of her name.) And no, I'm not going to the party. I'm not that far along this path. My blue dragon may be smaller than my white one, but he's still around on the look out for meals.

Buddha faced his negative emotions straight on. After that he ignored them and moved on, allowing them to die natural deaths. If he can, we can. It's your choice.

# Chapter Twenty-one

# Tenacity

Better than a hundred years of mischief
Is one day spent in contemplation.

Better than a hundred years of ignorance
Is one day spent in reflection.

Better than a hundred years of idleness
Is one day spent in determination.

Better to live one day
Wondering
How all things arise and pass away.

Better to live one hour
Seeing
The life beyond the way.

Better to live one moment
In the moment
Of the way beyond the way.

—The Dhammapada

It took the Buddha six years. He gave up everything, his family, his friends, everything he owned, his youth, and—almost—his life. It took him six years from the time he consciously set out on his spiritual path to reach a state of profound awakeness. Imagine how long our path will be if it is all we can do to steal fifteen minutes from our days to focus on our heart's real work. A long, long time.

When I first started to meditate I was struck by how quickly the stress in my life began to subside. Then I was struck by how long it took for it to go away completely—and I *still* have my moments. I could not believe how long it took for the ticker tape of thoughts parading in my head to slow down long enough for me to experience peace—that emptiness that is like a warm comforter surrounding my life. In fact, as I recall, I managed to make it all the way through my first year and a half in the seminary with a brain crammed full of planning, lust, and speech writing. I didn't realize how slow the going was until, in the middle of a meditation course, when our temple priest turned to me and asked: "How long did it take you before your thinking mind stopped?" Red-faced, I reported that it still hadn't happened, and I had been meditating for years.

But then things did change. I could tell because of subtle differences in the way I began to live my life. There wasn't as much anger, or if I did get angry, it was for shorter periods of time. My "insta-judge" thinking, which just had to have an opinion about everything, disappeared for long periods of time—occasionally for a whole afternoon. And space appeared between my thoughts when I sat in meditation. And I was happy.

It took years and it took tenacity. I realized one day that deciding to stumble along a spiritual path is like deciding to train for a marathon. We may need to start over a thousand times until it takes. Maybe more. Tenacity is about taking the time and making the commitment to start again. Over and over and over and over.

Tenacity. *The American Heritage Dictionary* defines it as "holding onto something persistently." Think glue. You've already made a decision to follow a spiritual path. How do I know? Because you never would have read this far if it wasn't true. There are simply too many other ways you could be using your time. Now, I have to tell you that the decision is the easy part. Sticking with it, as anyone who has decided to give up an addiction knows, could end up being the hardest thing you've ever done, but the most rewarding.

All religions that I know of are rich with stories of tenacity. And of advice. In ancient Korea there was a great fourteenth-century Zen adept known as T'aego, who was widely considered to be a true teacher of wisdom. It was a period in history when the Mongol empire was breaking down as communication linkages sprouted connecting China, Korea, Vietnam, and Japan. As a nation, Korea was struggling to rid itself of foreign control. Chaos ruled the day, with religious teachers often reminding people of the importance of staying true to their ethics and the precepts of Buddhism. As J. C. Cleary describes it in a book about T'aego, "The adepts of Buddhism were the core of enlightened teachers and sincere students who were not only seekers but finders. They knew Buddhism as a body of wisdom that was ancient in human historical terms, yet modern for being always currently engaged in a necessary course of renewal." T'aego was at the top of the pile. He was wise, feisty, blunt, modern, skillful, and tenacious. He was the teacher of his time, the man from whom all the later lineages of the Korean Zen chain ultimately descended. Born in 1301, he died in 1382, after spending most of his life teaching spiritual practices.

In many ways T'aego lived his life predictably. He was a seeker from the age of thirteen, traveling from Buddhist center to Buddhist center seeking wisdom. According to the history books, enlightenment came at age thirty-two. He emerged as a national figure in his fifties. It's his directness that makes him worth knowing. T'aego probably received thousands of visitors seeking wisdom. In one teaching he emphasized the importance of putting your whole heart into your practice, all the time: "Twenty-four hours a day, in the midst of whatever you are doing, just take this meditation saying as the root of life. Always be attentive: Examine it all the time. Put your attention on (it) and stick it in front of your eyes. Be like a hen sitting on her eggs to make sure they stay warm. Be like a cat waiting to catch a mouse....Just go on like this, more and more alert and clear, investigating closely, like an infant thinking of its mother, like someone hungry longing for food, like someone thirsty thinking of water. Rest, but do not stop." (*A Buddha from Korea: The Zen Teachings of T'aego*, translated with commentary by J. C. Cleary, Shambhala, Boston and Shaftesbury, 1988, p. xi-xii)

Rest, but do not stop. When I first met my teacher, Samu Sunim, I had been meditating for some time and thought of myself as extraordinarily advanced, given the amount of time I spent meditating each day (about a half hour). Ah, delusion. Small, lithe, with an easiness in his movements that belies the intensity of his personality and his drive to teach, Sunim has taught me the importance of not stopping. The first summer I knew him he had started to cruise Chicago on a hunt for a location for a third Zen temple, having nurtured healthy *sanghas* (Buddhist communities) in Toronto and Ann Arbor. Most of the rest of us resisted his enthusiasm, knowing that the seeding of a new temple would be hard, hard work. What optimists we turned out to be.

He found a building. It was quite a sight to behold—a wreck, a total wreck of four stories near the baseball park in the city. It was then a former home to a men's fraternal organization and current home of a Pentecostal Christian Church. It needed everything, and it turned out that the entire basement was covered—and I do mean covered—in sewage. Now here's tenacity. Sunim was unfazed. Work parties came from Toronto, from Ann Arbor, from anywhere. Donations trickled in from the existing Buddhist community in Chicago. Sunim made several begging trips to Korea. Centimeter by centimeter the building was transformed.

On one visit I spent days filling tiny holes in the walls. Other people removed the sewage, bucket by bucket. We painted and painted and painted and painted. Throughout, most of us whined: It was too much; there was no money; had Sunim gone crazy? We were depending on volunteers. Some people, rightfully exhausted, got angry and left. Others just left without warning. One day they were there—the next day they weren't. New people showed up. The whining continued. A whole winter passed without heat. I remember sleeping on a futon one night, fully clothed (complete with a hat, gloves, and socks) with six blankets over me, in a sleeping bag, still shivering through the coldest part of the night. For a long time there was no hot water. Sometimes there was no running water at all. Some of us said we just couldn't transform the building. Let's just go home. Sunim just kept going.

Today the building is magnificent. Its main meditation hall is a glorious high-ceilinged golden room with deep reds and blues, and an altar with three statues that draw you to them. It is an urban retreat center sitting in the middle of Chicago, open to anyone with a sincere heart. It exists because Sunim had the tenacity to just keep going, step after step. It was amazing to watch, and the whole experience taught me the power of sheer stick-to-it-ness.

Another living, breathing example of tenacity with passion is Susan Powter. I lost almost five hundred dollars when I prepaid for some aerobics classes at her Susan Powter Center, only to find the doors padlocked when I showed up for the first class. I love her anyway. Here's why: Susan Powter taught the public about fat. Other people knew about it, but she taught us by bringing it out of the scientific closet and turning it into rubber "fat glob" magnets we could stick on our refrigerators. But that's not why I love her. I love her because she has more tenacity than anyone I have ever met, with the possible exception of Michael Moore of "Roger and Me," and "T.V. Nation," fame. By the time she was a young mother of two and separated from her husband, Susan has told us all, she weighed 260 pounds. That is a whole lot of pounds. Two tiny kids. Lonely. Eating M&Ms at two-thirty AM with "Love Boat" reruns to keep her company. $1,400 a month income. Until, one day, she woke up and decided to change her life.

And change she did. First she went on a fast and took diet pills. Then she went on an eight-hundred calorie-a-day diet and lost weight. Then gained it back, again and again. She tried aerobics. That didn't work. So Susan started to walk. That's all. The first time she took her kids out to her front yard, parked them under a tree, and went for a walk half way down the block with her head turned watching the kids. She started to walk every day, seven days a week. Then she spent months as the "crazy fat lady in the back" of an aerobics class. Until she stepped on a scale at her father's home and saw 114 pounds. Most of us would have stopped there, figuring we had earned sufficient bragging rights to keep going for awhile. After all she had downsized by more than 130 pounds. But Susan figured if she could do it, we could do it, and proceeded to take on the entire diet industry to teach the rest of us a more sane approach to weight control. She has given years to this: Spicey Saint Susan.

Models of tenacity are everywhere if we look. Here's a story related to trees. During World War I, a Frenchman went off to war only to discover that his wife, who had worked for the French Underground, had been brutally murdered in his absence. His anguish was so deep that he went into the mountains to mourn her loss. At first he plotted revenge. But after some months he decided that he would spend the rest of his life making the earth a better place, in his wife's honor. He decided that he would make it his job to reforest the parts of France that had been devastated by the war. People laughed. He said he would plant a thousand acorns each day. The laughter continued until people realized how serious he was. Every day, for the rest of his life, he planted a thousand acorns. On some days he would be joined by school children. Today there are forests where his seeds were sewn. And "the tree man" is a national hero. Tenacity was what pulled the thread forward from a single action yesterday to a reforested mountain today.

So take the next step. That's all. You've come so far. Too far not to, really. And if you have to start your stumbling all over again a thousand times, then start a thousand times. If you need more, there's time.

# Chapter Twenty-two

# Relax, My Darling

*"The secret of living with frustration and worry
is to avoid becoming personally involved in your
own life."*
— The Great Bodhisattva, Ziggy

June 1996, marked the second anniversary of my moving into the Ann Arbor Zen Buddhist Temple as a full-time resident. To say I was living the frazzled life when I arrived is the understatement of my last decade. At the time I was deep in the throes of deciding that high-end management consulting was not, after all, my future and I had just sold the house of many people's dreams. It was a big brick, four-bedroomed two-fireplaced, two-kitchened monster of a building that stayed in shape by regularly suckling at my paychecks. Since I was letting go of the management consultant life and my home, it only seemed right to also give away everything I owned. So I did. Except my pictures, a desk, and a bookcase full of books.

Moving into the temple meant downsizing to where everything I and my then twelve-year-old daughter owned would fit into one 14 x 16-square-foot room. (This is a guess. It seemed that big anyway.) We managed. To make things even more complicated, a man who has been a friend of mine for almost twenty years showed up at the temple doorstep that summer—direct from Australia—to announce that I was, after all, the woman he wanted to spend the rest of his life with, even if it meant selling his Queensland-based construction business and moving into a Zen Buddhist Temple in Ann Arbor, Michigan. He later reneged, for excellent reasons all things considered. But I digress.

So there I was, furniture abandoned, house sold, corporate environment shunned, ready to live the life of a true monastic, even if my monastery was a Victorian house on the busiest street in town.

Somewhere back in time a very famous Zen master whose name completely eludes me, said that living in a temple magnifies every experience eighty-seven times—I think he underestimated by a lot. My initial experience was that I had shifted from purgatory to hell. Because I had to earn money to pay for our room and board and send monthly financial support to my mother, there was a need to continue to sell some consulting time. This was quite an adventure in itself. Imagine returning a phone call to someone who has recently begun to identify herself as the president of a small strategic planning consulting firm, only to hear a calm voice answering the phone, "The Zen Buddhist Temple" when you need to track her down. The temple had more hang ups during my residency than before or since. The good news was that those brave beings who stayed through the initial phone pick-up to ask for me, self-selected themselves, so I ended up with terrific clients. (Maybe I've discovered a new marketing strategy. To make certain that you only work with ethical companies who respect their workers and *always* pay their bills, find a church or religious organization to answer your phone for you.)

In the meantime, the temple's schedule was grueling. Since I was the most junior resident I was responsible for wake-up. That meant setting an alarm for four forty-five each morning, preparing the meditation hall, opening the temple for visitors, and chanting everyone else awake. Days were an endless stream of constant chores coupled with a gnawing sense of being "on call" to the universe. That meant dropping whatever it was I was doing if someone called or showed up at the temple doorstep to ask about Buddhism or to talk about a problem they were experiencing, either with their practice or in general. At the same time, just like Superman (but there the analogy ends), I would periodically stop in the middle of whatever it was I was doing, change into my royal blue power suit and go off to consult. It was quite a roller coaster.

Evening service, temple chores, and responsibilities related to being in the seminary rounded out the days which typically ended at eleven PM. It all started again at four forty-five the next morning.

After a few weeks I was wired. I was CRABBY. My thoughts were mean; the world was ugly. (And those were my good days.) In retrospect, I suspect that most of what I was experiencing was a combination of sleep deprivation and withdrawal from one of our culture's favorite drugs, Diet Coke, and it didn't help to be utterly without privacy.

Paramita Nat Needle was along beside me as a seminary student and nearby resident. Many times his words of encouragement were a source of inspiration, and watching him work through his own issues taught me that my reactions to temple life were not so unusual. Plus, he also did some of the chores around the temple when he was in Ann Arbor. Then he went away on a trip and I was miserable. My practice stank. I kept falling asleep or would sit on my cushion mentally listing all the wrongs done me from as far back as I could remember (three years of age). There were slews of them. I'm sure I made everyone around me quite unhappy, not that I ever had the courage to look. There was no peacefulness, no "one with everything-ness."

One day when Paramita came back from the trip, he asked me to meet him outside of the temple because he had found a perfect gift for me during his travels. It was a paperweight. One of those glass ball things that weigh about four pounds and have stuff on the bottom like shells or pretty stones. Mine had blue and green, yellow and orange paint splatters. And the words, "Relax my darling."

My whole experience changed. All I could do at first was stare at the paperweight not knowing whether I was going to laugh or cry. I think I laughed, and vowed to do just that—to relax. With that promise, all the angst and anxiety and exhaustion melted into gentleness, compassion, and respect which has stayed with me (mostly) until even now. My practice shifted to where moments on the cushion were deep peace. I discovered a stillness that has stayed with me through thick and thin. I discovered I could get through anything, even death, when I relaxed. Decisions became easier, my pace slowed, and I rediscovered my sense of humor.

A part of me figured that Buddha must have talked about this somewhere so I started rereading sutras looking for words of wisdom related to relaxing. And sure enough, he did. In the Dhammapada, some instructions: Four attitudes and actions foster an ability to relax into our spiritual work—delighting in meditation, delighting in solitude, holding our tongues, and embracing whatever happens to us.

More easily said than done, however. Those lucky souls who already know how to relax as they meditate will also tell you that they delight in meditation. Unfortunately for those of us who have lost the art of relaxation, delighting in anything is hard. Amy Gross, the editor of *Elle*, calls it the lament of the Filofax slave: "You talk fast and carry a thick Filofax. An unstructured day is an invitation to chaos. A few minutes of free time could drive you nuts with its potential uses. I race through my life leading with my left wrist (the better to see my watch), my right hand clutching my date book. As I used to ask my mother if I could play with my friend, I now ask my Filofax. It is a merciless disciplinarian, its pages insisting that I schedule events from eight in the morning to eight at night. It tells me that I only have one lunch slot free in the next four weeks. Unless someone cancels." *(Elle,* June, 1996, Editor's page.) Sound familiar?

Buddha didn't even bother to say, "Relax." Instead, he aimed his arrow sideways by suggesting specific actions that would naturally lead to a relaxed life, an experience of the day-to-day as art, filled with inspiration and creativity, play, and even delight. None of these are possible, or were possible for me when I was living my day as an anxious, knotted-up, goal-driven, seminary student/consultant. Buddha's first words of encouragement, to delight in meditation, comes with lots of later coaching from many Zen masters. Hakuin, a sixteenth-century Japanese teacher, used to tell his students that three actions would lead them to experience of delight in meditation. First he urged them, and us, to *"have faith in our practice."* For me this has meant continuing to meditate every day, day in and day out, when at least half the time I want desperately to be doing something else. It has meant that I've chosen to believe that there will be benefits derived from spiritual practice, even if they aren't immediately obvious. This is the kind of faith you see in little kids climbing a slide for the first time, certain that their parent will be there to catch them even when they see them talking to someone else as they climb the slide's stairs. And sure enough their parents are at the bottom of that slide at the precise moment when, if they weren't, the kid would end up face down in the dirt. That's the kind of faith we need—little kid faith.

Hakuin's second piece of advice was to *"keep a ball of doubt"* growing in our practice. In other words we need to question, question, question. What is this all about? What is life? What is it that keeps us going? What? My own ball of doubt is the feeling that I'm right on the edge of solving some unknown crime, and if I just keep meditating and believe in the practice, the crime will be solved.

Like anything else in life that we have decided to master, only to discover how tedious the work of building our new skill is, staying on target takes tenacity. That summer in the temple I told myself I was fed up at least a hundred times each day, sometimes more. But I kept hearing Hakuin's voice telling me to have faith. To be honest, I knew that the lifestyle and big house and consulting profession had left me feeling empty in the deepest parts of me. Hakuin taught that *tenacity* is the third action. Without it we will desert spiritual work after a string of frustrating days and our concentration will slowly dry up like a water table that isn't replenished. Our faith and ball of doubt keep us tenacious and vice versa. We need to keep at it. That's what we did to learn how to walk, to run, to ride our bikes, to swim. To a person, masters of any art or skill talk about this. It's how they got to where they are today. Jessye Norman, the opera star, will tell you that she had this voice inside of her head that would say, "Just keep going, Jessye," whenever she would falter. Annie Dillard in *The Writing Life*, expresses it in a different way: "Jack London claimed to write twenty hours a day...once he had a book of his own under way, he set his alarm to wake him after four hours sleep....The long poem, John Berryman said, takes between five and ten years. Thomas Mann was a prodigy of production. Working constantly, he wrote a page a day." Flaubert finished a book every five to seven years. A full-time writer averages a book every five years. Seeing those five years through to the finish line is what I'm talking about. If we keep the faith, roll our balls of doubt, and stay tenacious about our spiritual drive, sooner or later we'll discover that we do, after all, delight in meditation.

There's more. Buddha urged us to delight in solitude as a way to reach "sublime relaxation." We say we enjoy solitude already, but we don't. For example, how many of us drive our cars in silence, radio free? When do we take time to be alone in our days? I remember a psychologist asking me how much time I took for myself in a given day. At the time I was a graduate student and full-time mother, and believed that I did have alone time every day. After all, I wasn't racing somewhere to punch a clock and at least one of the kids took naps. The therapist suggested that I track my days for two weeks "just to see." She believed that all of us need a daily minimum of fifteen minutes just for ourselves, to stay healthy, productive, and happy. I was stunned by the results which, as you might guess, showed no "me" time at all. I, of course, finding a "new religion" talked several nonbelieving friends into going through the same exercise. To their utter dismay they found they had no downtime in their days either.

Delight in solitude. Right now many of us don't even know what we would do with it if we had it. I sure didn't when I first started giving myself my own fifteen minutes each day. For years I used it for more sleep. Later it turned into a walk. Most recently it's saved for writing in a journal or reading sutras. It hasn't been easy to do, but it's been worth it. Someone once said that God is in the silence. If we have no silence, no solitude, how can we ever experience the divine, our own Buddha nature. The truth of the matter is that we can't. Period. Solitude seems to be the most difficult for people who come from a big, overachieving, workaholic family. I flat out had no idea how to embrace solitude when I first committed to making space in my day for some. To tell you the truth, I had to learn from books. I have probably read dozens of books on solitude by now (yes, there really are that many—which means I am not alone in this.) Most of the books are biographies: Jack London, May Sarton, Gertrude Stein, Thoreau, Annie Dillard. May Sarton ended up being my favorite coach, mostly because she struggled with solitude the way many of us do. In her *Journal of a Solitude*, she tells us, "I'm trying to do it by not hurrying, by not allowing the pressure to build. One step at a time. It is like climbing out of a deep well."

Buddha added more instructions. "Hold your tongue." Ah, if only we did. Of course this makes so much sense on paper. If we hold our tongues then we don't have to writhe over what we may have said that was hurtful or foolish. Without the writhing we can relax into our spiritual work. Who hasn't spent days, maybe more, suffering internally from words we wish had never leapt from our mouths? Some of us spend years beating ourselves up over something we said. I know I do.

When he was asked to explain this advice, Buddha told his followers to think three times before they said anything, ever. If, after that, they were still unsure, he told them to think about it ten times. Imagine what the world would be like if we thought about what we were going to say before we said anything. Think of the marriages that would be saved. E-mail would probably drop off by eighty percent. Whole forests could be saved. I'm sure we would still find someone yelling at us, or giving us the finger on the road, every once in awhile, but the regularity would go away, don't you think?

This piece of advice always hits me hardest when I'm on retreats. Maybe it's because my observing mind is most conscious of what I'm experiencing in the silence of retreat. I can tell you that thinking about something ten times has saved me many a relationship. In one of the first retreats I ever led I had a terrible time with one of the men who was participating. He is very bright and has been practicing Buddhism much longer than I. He can recite whole sutras and has memorized our patriarchal lineage which is akin to memorizing whole pages of a telephone directory. He knows all the rituals cold. I'm telling you the man is good at this, really good.

I, on the other hand, mostly remember the rituals I learned in the seminary unless I am under pressure to perform (self-induced suffering I know, but it's my reality at times). Such as in a retreat situation. When he is in the meditation hall, I always feel pressure. At times he will openly contradict an instruction I give, and frankly, when he does, his correction is usually right, and, to be even more honest, helpful. At this particular retreat there was a woman attending who was exhausted, both physically and emotionally. The temple priest had asked me to single her out during the period of manual work, to tell her to rest, or if she preferred, to do some solitary practice in the meditation hall. When I went looking for her, this fellow had asked her to help him do the work he had been assigned. When I motioned to her to follow me, he stopped what he was doing and told me that he had asked her to help him. When I responded that she was needed to do something else, he looked at me and rolled his eyes the way we all did as little kids when our parents repeated some lecture we had already heard hundreds of times. You know what I mean. That "I-don't-want-to-hear-this-but-I-know-I-have-to-stand-here-and-listen-to-you" roll of the eyes.

I could feel my face flush with anger. It was bad enough that I was watching every move I made in the meditation hall myself. It was bad enough when I forced myself to admit when he had been right correcting me. And now this. It was all I could do to just walk away. One: When I saw him again twenty minutes later I was still mad. Two: As we entered the mediation hall for a sitting and words of encouragement (by yours truly) I wanted to use him as an example of what not to do. Three: I didn't. But I was still mad. So I kept counting, kept watching my thoughts. At ten, and only at ten, could I let go and complete the retreat with some grace. You can guess the punch line. At the end he told me how moving the retreat was. I just cringed, remembering how much of it I had wasted on my own reaction to his gesture. I realized that, for me, his job is to find my raw spots, my insecurities, and rub them until they no longer exist, until I can fully see how I am the one creating my own reactions. He just helps set the stage, as only a true dharma brother can. Which is not to say that I wasn't utterly relieved that the retreat finally ended. I was.

And finally, to relax, we need to literally embrace all that happens to us. There was a recent article in, I think it was *The National Enquirer,* which reported that aliens had put microchips into all of our brains to see what we spent our time thinking about. After a few short weeks they took them back out because they were exhausted by all of our whining. It seems that a very few of us are satisfied with our lot. We keep wanting more; a bigger house, a thinner body, a grander pay check, happier kids or parents. As long as we're whining we can't relax. Not ever. As Sinead O'Connor says, "I don't want what I haven't got." I agree with her attitude. If you only have eight crayons in your box, then make the best picture you can without wasting any time thinking that everyone else has more. They aren't you, and you may have more talent with two crayons than all the rest of us with thousands. We need to want what we have and to be deeply grateful for whatever it is because it's the compost that will grow us into roses. It is what is making us wise.

Master Sheng-yen's words of encouragement, spoken in a 1983 summer retreat, repeats this same message: "My advice for people who are afraid of or do not like the heat is this—take a large dose of it." In that same retreat, he reminded participants of a method of spiritual practice that is apparently still prevalent in the East. Spiritual seekers purposefully make a pilgrimage to famous monasteries during the hottest part of the year. But here's the clincher. They don't just walk to a monastery; they do a prostration after every third step. As you can imagine, a pilgrimage can take the entire summer. Picture yourself walking to the nearest supermarket, with the commitment to do a prostration every third step. Other than being wildly entertaining to anyone who noticed you, it would take an incredibly long time. For me, it would be a day, maybe longer, and I would be so sore I would probably take a cab home. These pilgrims spend weeks, months even. A summer of heat, sand, and dirt. A summer coated in dust and filled with thirst. What happens to them along the way is something to watch. To complete the pilgrimage they have to learn to accept "what is." They can't afford to be anxious or expect anything, when they know that they will be doing prostrations in all kinds of weather, under all sorts of conditions.

When you talk to someone who has been through this type of a pilgrimage they will tell you that they learn to take one prostration at a time, knowing that if they allowed themselves to think about what it will take to complete what they set out to do, or how far they have yet to go, they would become overwhelmed by frustration, anxiety, and discouragement. If they allowed their minds to whine about the weather they would give up after a day or two. So they simply accept each moment. "You have to reach a state where you have no thoughts of bodily or mental discomfort...the hot weather is an obstacle to your practice, but how large an obstacle it becomes is up to you...don't worry about your sweat and body odor. This isn't a job and I'm not a boss you have to impress. I'm not your date....If other people's smells and behavior bother you, that's your problem. If it bothers you to think that your smell might be bothering others, that again is your problem." ("Practice and Hot Weather," by Master Sheng-yen, *Ch'an* Magazine, Volume 11, #3, Elmhurst, New York, p. 8)

So relax, my darling. Relax. When you do, your practice will deepen immeasurably. Your heart will open wider. Your wisdom eye will function better and the people around you will start asking who you've fallen in love with. You'll discover the art, the joyous art, of every day living. Bring to it all the qualities of an artist...bring it inspiration, concentration, play. That's it. Play with it. Play with your life, knowing the precious quality of each and every moment.

# Chapter Twenty-three

# Living Your Life as a True Master

---

*"Be happy about your growth, in which of course you can't take anyone with you, and be gentle with those who stay behind; be confident and calm in front of them and don't torment them with your doubts and don't frighten them with your faith or joy, which they wouldn't be able to comprehend. Seek out some simple and true feeling of what you have in common with them, which doesn't necessarily have to alter when you yourself change again and again; when you see them, love life in a form that is not your own and be indulgent toward those who are growing old, who are afraid of the aloneness that you trust. Avoid providing material for the drama that is always stretched tight between parents and children; it uses up much of the children's strength and wastes the love of the elders.... Believe in a love that is being stored up for you like an inheritance, and have faith that in this love there is a strength and a blessing so large that you can travel as far as you wish without having to step outside it."*

—(Rainier Maria Rilke, *Letters to a Young Poet,* translated and with a forward by Stephen Mitchell, First Vintage Books, Random House, New York, 1986, pp. 42-43)

---

You've become your own master. And while teachers may be helpful, your job is to follow the wisdom and compassion that have emerged out of your own practice. *Trust yourself.*

In all the wonderful characters who surrounded the Buddha, Ananda really is one of my all-time favorites. Not just because he was at the receiving end of an obsession with desire, but because he was a whiner too—but in a good way. And he was a nag—also in a good way. I think of him as a patron saint since it was his nagging at the Buddha which finally—after three rounds of mega-nagging—caused the Buddha to allow the acceptance of women into the monk realm. So he's my guy. Anyway, Ananda got whinier and whinier as Buddha was dying. He wanted him to name a successor, which Buddha simply refused to do, even as his cousin Devadatta kept plotting to kill him in true Shakespearean fashion. Devadatta was determined to be the next spiritual leader of the sangha. So there was a ton of pressure on Buddha to name someone—if only to save his own life—but he wouldn't. Because, in the end, we are our own masters, you and I.

Once when his students came to him utterly confused about which spiritual teachers to believe, to trust, Buddha gave them guidelines which are as useful today as they were twenty-five-hundred years ago. In the Buddhist scriptures they are called "The Kalama Sutta."

1. Do not believe in anything on mere hearsay.
2. Do not believe in traditions merely because they are old and have been handed down for many generations and in many places.
3. Do not believe anything on account of rumors or because people talk a great deal about it.
4. Do not believe because the written testimony of some ancient sage is shown to you.
5. Do not believe in what you have fancied, thinking that, because it is extraordinary, it must have been inspired by a god or other wonderful being.
6. Do not believe anything merely because presumption is in its favor, or because the custom of many years inclines you to take it as true.

7. Do not believe anything merely on the authority of your teachers and priests.

But whatsoever, after thorough investigation and reflection, is found to agree with reason and experience, as conducive to the good and benefit of one and all and of the world at large; that only accept as true, and shape your life in accordance therewith. Buddha said that these guidelines needed to be applied to his own teachings: "Do not accept any doctrine from reverence, but first try it as gold is tried by fire."

You need to trust your own wisdom and to learn from your own experience. In many ways this is much harder than having someone else tell us what to do or what to believe. When you trust yourself you'll find that there are few absolutes. Maybe none. That's why judgment is so dangerous. Every situation which makes you deeply uncomfortable deserves your unwavering concentration. If you need to make a serious decision, just sit with it. Think through the pros and cons with as little emotion as you can, then just let go. And sit. In the silence will come the decision—whether you like it or not.

Years ago I was deep in the throes of a most excellent love affair. My partner was this gorgeous contractor, who was smart and funny. The only problem was that our values clashed in the noisiest way possible. While we agreed on how most, if not all, of the problems in this society have surfaced, our solutions were on different planets. Where I wanted to focus on trying to integrate kindness and concern for each other into existing systems, his view was that the government and our major institutions are utterly corrupted and that we would all be best served if they were downsized to where every Libertarian in the country would be pleased. (The older I get the more I think he may have been right, but too late now.) And we were both lousy fighters. He sulked and I would end the relationship at least once every two weeks because of something he had done. We were locked in a painful embrace that neither of us knew how to get out of.

The last straw was when we went camping with some friends of his. It was a disaster from the moment we met up with them. He stopped talking to me midway through the weekend. Trust me when I say that most humans walking the earth today would have stopped talking to me midway through. I was nasty; tired nasty; bitch nasty. I had no idea what to do, we were both so miserable. Yet the physical attraction was strong, and when we were in sync we were America's happiest couple.

So I sat. I wished I had a teacher to talk to, but we were in Michigan's upper peninsula, easily six hundred miles from the nearest teacher I could think of. All I had was me. First I cried; that took about an hour. Then I felt sorry for myself; add two more hours. Then I did a pro and con list of whether we could really be together in my own head. To be honest, I was leaning toward the "we can make it work" side of the page. Finally, I just sat. And sat. And sat. After what felt like days (it was probably an hour or so), there was this little voice that kept saying, "Only love him, Only love him." My initial reaction was pleased. We would work it out. But the voice said, "No, silly, *not together*. Just love him. You can't stay with him. You would both be miserable in the long run." Ugh. I was not a happy camper, but any way I looked at the solution, it came out as the wisest move for us both. So we parted friends. We are to this day, in spite of some hiccups along the way. I have to admit that it's comforting to know he's out there, living his life, taking on corruption where he finds it, as only he can.

Don't believe anything on mere hearsay. Respecting traditions is one thing, believing in them without the benefit of your own reaction to them is not so wise. Forget rumors. Fads fade. And don't get caught up in thinking you have all the answers because you don't. Besides, the right answer in this moment can easily be the wrong answer in the next one. Question authority—all authority. That does not mean that we need to defile or destroy authority. Every society, every culture, needs ground rules and focal points and someone needs to police them—hopefully with sufficient checks and balances in place so we don't all end up revolutionaries.

When something strikes you as right, even after you've reflected on it at length, even after you've meditated or prayed, and when it promotes the well being, not just of the people and things nearby, but of the rest of the world, well then it probably is right. You'll know. You are your own master.

A dangerous time this—the first taste of deep knowing, of deep security. The way you live your life will be important. A true master takes care of himself or herself. As I reflect back on the teachers I've known, I've been struck by the similarities in their lifestyles. They sleep. They take time to rest. I don't think I've met a single one who is a "night person." Most seem to go to bed early (ten or eleven PM) and wake up early (five or six AM). They eat healthy food, but not too much of it. They actually like vegetables and fruits. (One of my teachers' favorite breakfast foods is steamed kale. It takes some getting used to with oatmeal, but once you acquire the taste you miss it when it isn't on the table.)

They stay away from television for the most part and may see a few movies a year, as special occasions. Quiet surrounds them. They move with grace and with humor. Even when there is a crisis, there is always a calmness about them which reaches past the crisis into a sky of wisdom, where they choose their reaction to the situation.

And if something is unclear they turn to the dharma—to the teachings, to the wisdom—that all of the great teachers left as a legacy. The Eightfold Path. *The Sermon on the Mount. The Dhammapada. The Koran. The I Ching.* It's all there, waiting to be tapped, happy to be of use.

These writings nourish us. They remind us to be confident in our stumbling, to trust it. They give us energy and teach us about mindfulness. And they are chock-full of clues that unfold the mystery of spiritual growth. They also warn us about the behaviors that can knock us to our knees, like abusing drugs and alcohol, partying too heartily, gambling, spending time in "places of depravity," and hanging out with people of poor character. They tell us laziness is more destructive than we expect. A good bout of laziness can lift you right off the path and head-first into the bramble patch. For some of us, one taste of understanding and we start referring to ourselves as "Dalai Lama West" under our breath. It's easy to forget that this path is ongoing, and that understanding deepens with continued practice.

Buddha's last words were to live by the teachings—by the dharma, by the exquisite intersection of wisdom and compassion—and not let up: "Be diligent in your efforts to attain liberation."

Be diligent. That's all. Keep at it and everything else will take care of itself.

This then, is mastery: diligence in practice. Because where there is a deep abiding spirituality, there is wisdom and compassion. There is thoughtfulness, reflection, clarity. There is a willingness to take responsibility for one's own life and to understand, as completely as possible, why we are as we are. This mastery is not mistake-free. It is simply ever-deepening. Without greed, there is an absence of lust for power, and so wise decisions can be made. Without anger, the need for revenge dissipates. Instead, empathy and visions of possibilities arise; energy surges.

There is work to be done. You are your own master. What will you do with your life?

# Chapter Twenty-four

# On Community

---

*Friendship is more than acquaintance and it involves more than affection. Friendship usually arises out of mutual interests and common aims, and these pursuits are strengthened by the benevolent impulses that sooner or later grow. The demands of friendship for frankness, for self-revelation, for taking criticisms as seriously as expressions of admiration or praise, for stand-by-me-loyalty, and for assistance to the point of self-sacrifice—are all potent encouragements to moral maturation and even ennoblement.*

—(*The Book of Virtues: A Treasury of Great Moral Stories,* edited by William J. Bennett. Simon & Schuster, New York, 1993, p. 269).

---

Friendship writ large is community.

So. It is the last day of your life. You look back. What meant the most to you? Where did you find joy? Which rocks hid from you? Who helped you? Where was your energy best spent? Please remember that life is very, very short and every moment is the most precious moment you have. Keep your strides strong and your focus sharp.

In the dead of winter in 1971, Pan American Flight 12 took off from Washington, D.C.'s Dulles Airport bound for London. It was filled with people from Britain, Germany, America, India, and the Middle East.

Among them was a young American copywriter/songwriter who was headed for Europe to do some commercials for Coca Cola.

The plane never landed in London. The fog was so thick that the plane finally had to land late in the afternoon in Shannon, Ireland. As the two hundred passengers got off the plane they discovered that there was only one small motel nearby, so they had to share rooms. At first, there was considerable resistance. Several refused, choosing to spend the night sleeping upright in the motel's lobby. The others paired themselves off as best they could by nationality and sex. Nobody knew how long they would be there. The songwriter missed his meeting.

The next day the passengers were asked to remain in the airport in case the weather cleared enough to take off for London. By midmorning the group, strangers twenty-four hours earlier, had formed small groups in the airport's small coffee shop. The common language was English. The common drink, Coca Cola. People from many different countries and cultures were sharing drinks and stories and forming community, keeping each other company. "He was watching a composite of the whole world reforming around him in new groups, based not so much on national boundaries or common business interests as on a desire to keep company with someone else." And one of the most famous jingles of all time started to take form. The young man wrote on a paper napkin, "I'd like to buy the world a Coke and keep it company." (Bill Backer, *The Care and Feeding of Ideas,* Times Books, New York and Toronto, 1993, pp. 6-8)

We are *all* thirsty for community. All of us. A supportive community, a *sangha,* can support us when we falter and remind us of our quest for spiritual knowledge. And we can return the favor. Like a broken record, Buddha reminded his disciples to trust him, the teachings, and each other; to trust community.

Like little tigers, we are each hungry for community, for belonging. We want to be a member of a group of people with shared values and concerns, a group of people who see it as part of their life purpose to help each other however they can. This yearning shows itself in infinite ways. Several months ago I discovered it at a McDonalds in Midland, Michigan at seven AM on a Saturday, morning when I suddenly found

228

myself surrounded by eight elderly men who had been meeting there every Saturday morning for quite some time. Since I had unknowingly plunked myself down in the middle of the group I became an honorary member. We talked about weather, football, their wives (several were dead), and how times change. The next day, I enjoyed similar conversations at a church. The day after that a corporation's annual luncheon hosted the same themes. Friends who participated in the Million Man March in 1996, still talk about how emotionally powerful the experience of community was for them. We *want* community. At the same time, many of us, myself included, have forgotten in our busyness what it takes to create a community which feeds our yearning to be a part of something bigger than ourselves.

To maintain your spiritual momentum, it is helpful to create a spiritual community around yourself which affirms your efforts. No, I don't mean that we need to go out and create ashrams or new towns. You can start where you are, with the people you know.

What is community really? More than simply offering a sense of belonging, a genuine community has particular characteristics. First, it is inclusive. In other words, all are welcome. All faiths, all colors, all shapes, all sizes, all sexes. No one is left out. And individuals' differences are welcomed and even celebrated, not ignored, denied, hidden, or changed. Second, a community is realistic. Community is not nirvana: In fact, part of being a member of a community is being willing to face problems with all the players around the table. People listen, really listen to each other. No one is rejected. Conflict doesn't have to be resolved with physical or emotional bloodshed. Instead it is resolved with our emerging wisdom and grace and a view to the greater good. Third, a community cares for its members. We take care of each other knowing that each and every one of us is as precious as a drop of water to a thirsty camel. How can we do less?

Real communities examine themselves regularly for evidence of anger, greed, or delusion. This self-examination, in its truest sense, builds community. Because the greed, anger, and delusion can be stemmed and, over time, be reconfigured as compassion, loving kindness, equanimity, joy—but you already knew that.

A healthy community is a safe community. These days, in spite of the press touting lowered crime rates, it is rare to feel safe, particularly for women and children. We need to give a feeling of safety back to each other, and to protect each other, to step in, especially when we think someone might be physically threatened. In such a community we take responsibility for ourselves, and our own behavior. Each of us has a role to play, from keeping an eye on the children in the neighborhood, to volunteering, to leading a support group. We forget about the capacity of each of us to do good work. Community provides us with an outlet for just that.

And celebration matters. In a real community we work, *and* we play. We care for each other and the earth, *and* we celebrate. We laugh. We sing. We cry. We feel all of our emotions. We are eager participants in life and in sharing our life with the other members of the community.

In so many ways, a community that works is an ongoing witness to our spiritual "progress," our intelligence, our courage, our persistence. Community makes it possible for its members to slowly but surely develop a capacity to confirm and appreciate one another, as brothers and sisters. Without this capacity, our suffering will only worsen and more and more members of our larger community will be lost. Already forty thousand children die of hunger each day. How can we live with this truth? Without community, more and more of us could isolate ourselves to "save our own." Families lose when this happens. So will children. So will we all.

And the size of this community? The world of course. This is a community of all of us, for all of us. All faiths, all colors, all shapes, all sizes, all sexes. No one is left out. We need to take care of each other knowing that each and every one of us is as precious as a drop of water to a thirsty camel. How can we do less?

Every act, however small, will have an impact. Of this there is no doubt. And in the doing, a community will form of fellow stumblers with opening hearts, sparkling eyes, and if you're really lucky, wild life-giving humor. Who will be your allies? Spiritual teachers have told us and Buddha was downright blunt:

*"It should be known that there are four kinds of good-hearted friends who are worthy to be associated with. They are the following, namely:*

1. *The good-hearted one who will render you help.*
2. *The good-hearted one who will participate in your wealth and woe with the same feelings as his own.*
3. *The good-hearted one who will cause the advancement of your prosperity.*
4. *The good-hearted one who will ever have compassion towards you."*

These are the people who will look out for you, console you, give you more than you ask for. They will keep your secrets and will not desert you in times of need. They will help you keep the precepts, your word, and your head when those old foes anger, greed, and delusion decide to check out your neighborhood. They are earth angels and fortunately, they are all around us.

So get out there and build community. To start, be kind—always be kind. Watch for ways to be helpful. Participate in spiritual activities. Listen. Meditate. Pray. Protect children whenever and however you can. Honor the elderly; their wisdom can be deep and their guidance helpful. And slow down. *Slow down.* Building community is no more than these things at its core. Not massive projects. No federal grants. Ordinary actions from ordinary people—this, then, is our mandate, our life's work. To grow ourselves spiritually until we know, in our bones, that the whole world really is our home. It's time to take care of it, time to make it safe, time to make it whole, time to sing in perfect harmony.